CREATIVE PLANNIN   FS

Pirates and the Seaside

Lucy Peet

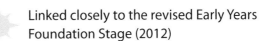

- Linked closely to the revised Early Years Foundation Stage (2012)

- Six weeks of differentiated planning

- Coverage across the 7 areas and 17 aspects of learning

- Activities based upon Playing and Exploring, Active Learning, Creating and Thinking Critically

- Guidance on assessing characterisitics of learning

Published 2012 by Featherstone Education
Bloomsbury Publishing Plc
50 Bedford Square, London, WC1B 3DP
www.bloomsbury.com

ISBN 978-1-4081-7395-4

Text © Lucy Peet 2012
Design © Lynda Murray
Photographs © Shutterstock

Printed in Great Britain by Latimer Trend & Company Ltd

10 9 8 7 6 5 4 3 2 1

This book is produced using paper that is made from wood grown in
managed, sustainable forests. It is natural, renewable and recyclable.
The logging and manufacturing processes conform to the environmental
regulations of the country of origin.

To see our full range of titles visit www.bloomsbury.com

Contents

About the series

This book is part of a series written for all who work with children in the Foundation Stage (FS). Owing to the fun, practical nature of the activities it is suitable for a wide range of settings, including schools, pre-schools, childminders and nurseries. Given that all the activities are differentiated for children working towards the Early Learning Goals (ELGs) 'the knowledge, skills and understanding children should have at the end of the academic year in which they turn five' (p.2, 2012), it is particularly relevant to practitioners working with FS1, FS2 and mixed-age classes. However, with the increasing good practice of the FS extending into Year 1 and 2 this book is invaluable for teachers wishing to promote active learning and a creative curriculum with children up to the age of seven. Each activity links with the requirements and expectations of the National Curriculum, statutory for Key Stage 1 in England and Wales, and through observation it will also be possible to collect evidence for Assessing Pupils' Progress. The table below shows the corresponding year groups for children from Scotland and Northern Ireland.

Year groups and corresponding ages:

Age	School year		
	England and Wales	**Scotland**	**Northern Ireland**
2 - 3	Foundation Stage		
3 - 4	FS1 (previously nursery)		P 1
4 - 5	FS2 (previously reception)	Primary 1	P 2
5 - 6	Year 1	Primary 2	P 3
6 - 7	Year 2	Primary 3	P 4

How this book is structured

Through the topic of pirates children will be involved in playing and exploring, active learning and creating and thinking critically: all key features of the revised Early Years Foundation Stage (EYFS) (2012). This book contains six weeks of planning – five weeks of detailed plans, with an activity designed for each specific area of learning, and a celebratory week of activity to share with parents and carers at the end covering the 'prime areas of learning'. Details are shown in the six week planning overview grid on page 62.

Activities are structured to build upon children's skills over the six weeks developing their experiences and abilities. For example, week 1 introduces a mathematical activity making and reading a map. This knowledge is extended in week 4 when the children use co-ordinates to locate items hidden under a cloth. Similarly, the investigation in week 2 into how much cargo a boat can carry before sinking is extended and consolidated in week 4 when the children consider different types of boat and build a boat of their own.

Through this method of extending similar tasks at a later date children are able to consolidate their knowledge and practise their skills. The final week of celebration is an opportunity to share the topic with parents and carers.

Each activity is clearly structured, with suggestions for:

♦ Resources required with relevant storybook or non-fiction book suggestions to support the main idea

♦ Key vocabulary

♦ A simple 'what to do' explanation with ideas for both guided and independent activity

♦ Differentiation of the activity at three levels. Each activity is pitched at an average level of understanding in line with the expected level of the ELGs. There are also ideas to **support** children who are working at the emerging stage and to **extend** children who are exceeding the ELGs. This clear differentiation ensures that all children in the group are exploring new ideas and concepts at a level appropriate to their stage of development. The Statutory Framework for the Early Years Foundation Stage states that (p.11) 'Practitioners must indicate whether children are meeting expected levels of development, or if they are exceeding expected levels, or not yet reaching expected levels. This is the EYFS Profile. The extension activities in this book are planned in line with the National Curriculum, ensuring that the children are building a firm foundation for Years 1 and 2.

♦ How to extend the activity throughout the week, with suggestions on how to deliver the activity as a **guided** session and ideas on how to encourage the children to work **independently**. The Statutory Framework for the Early Years Foundation Stage recognises that there is an important balance between activities led by children and activities led or guided by adults. It is important that 'each area of learning and development must be implemented through planned, purposeful play and through a mix of adult-led and child-initiated activity' (p.6, 2012). Each activity in this book includes guidance for practitioners as to how this balance can be achieved.

♦ Ideas for interactive display within the setting

♦ Ideas for parents and carers to use at home

Parents and carers as partners

Parents and carers are crucial in developing and supporting children's learning. This is recognised in the revised EYFS, and a key recommendation from the Tickell Review is that (p.18) '...the Government increases the emphasis within the EYFS on the role of parents and carers as partners in their children's learning...'. Indeed, the *Statutory Framework for the Early Years Foundation Stage* (March 2012) states that (p.2) 'Good parenting and high quality early learning together provide the foundation children need to make the most of their abilities and talents as they grow up'. The planning in this book includes an entire week based around inviting parents and carers into the setting to share in their children's curiosity and enthusiasm for learning. There are examples of how parents and carers can extend the learning at home, and ideas for giving parents and carers the opportunity not only to see what activities their children have been involved in, but also for them to join in alongside their children and to be really 'hands on'! One of the features which the EYFS seeks to provide (p.2, 2012) is 'partnership working between practitioners and with parents and/or carers'. This book recognises this as a priority.

Outdoor learning

Most of the activities are more than suitable to be engaged with outdoors as well as in a classroom – indeed for some of the activities it is necessary to be outdoors! And for some very messy, noisy or extensive activities I would recommend setting up outdoors to save carpets and soft furnishings and to minimise disruption to the rest of the learning environment. Hardly any of the activities require the children to sit and write in a formal situation. Where there is a suggestion to record, it is done either by an adult on a flipchart, children on individual whiteboards or pictorially, or through ICT, for example by the children using a digital camera or making a sound recording.

The revised curriculum

It is four years since the EYFS was introduced to provide a framework for all children in early years settings. The Tickell Report (2011) was carried out as an evaluation of the EYFS on children's outcomes and on those people working in the early years. One of the recommendations from the Tickell Report (2011) was that…

> …the assessment at the end of the EYFS, the EYFS Profile, should be significantly slimmed down and made much more manageable, based upon [my] 17 proposed new early learning goals…

The themes, principles and commitments of the EYFS remain the same, however the fourth theme, Learning and development has changed. This is the focus of our *Creative Planning in the EYFS* series. The *Statutory Framework for the Early Years Foundation Stage* (March 2012) states that one of the overarching principles which should shape practice in early years settings (p.3) is that 'children develop and learn in different ways and at different rates.' This book shows how topic-based activities can be provided in an exciting and practical way whilst still offering opportunities for all children at three levels of differentiation.

The research studied for the Tickell Report (2011) focuses on the concept that some aspects of development and learning include developing abilities, enabling children to be successful in all areas. These are referred to as 'prime areas of learning' and development. Other areas of learning are more specific to areas of knowledge and skills, these are known as 'specific areas of learning and development'.

Prime areas of learning and development

1. Communication and language

2. Physical development

3. Personal, social and emotional development

Specific areas of learning and development

1. Literacy

2. Mathematics

3. Understanding the world

4. Expressive arts and design

The activities in this book are planned around the four specific areas of learning and development – Literacy (formerly Communication, Language and Literacy), Mathematics (formerly Problem Solving, Reasoning and Numeracy), Understanding the World (formerly Knowledge and Understanding of the World) and Expressive Arts and Design (formerly Creative Development). However, the three prime areas are also covered through discussion, speaking and listening, turn taking and involvement in each task. It is essential that the prime and specific areas are planned for and experienced at the same time. They are not to be experienced chronologically but as an interwoven fabric of early years provision, as 'all areas of learning and development are important and inter-connected' (p.4, 2012).

Development in the prime areas has been called by neuroscientists 'experience expectant learning'. This is where a child's brain is ready to respond to interaction and stimulus, developing connections. Development in the specific areas however, will only develop when the need occurs, and includes cultural concepts such as learning to read and write, understand numbers, the number system and maps. This has been referred to as 'experience dependent learning'. (Hall, 2005).

The revisions made in the EYFS separate out the four strands of speaking, listening, reading and writing identified in the Rose Review (2006) into two areas: Communication and language (prime area) and Literacy (specific area). The Tickell Report (2011) explains this:

> …the development of communication and language skills happens during an optimum window of brain development and is experience expectant (therefore...prime)…whereas the acquisition of literacy skills is experience dependent since it can occur at any point in childhood or adulthood. (p.98)

As communication, language and literacy is so inextricably linked I have used ELGs from both these areas in the detailed differentiated activities.

Further reading

Hall, John (February 2005) **Neuroscience and Education – A review of the contribution of brain science to teaching and learning** *Research Report No.121* Scottish Council for Research in Education

Rose, Jim (March 2006) **Independent review of the teaching of early reading** *Final report* Department for Education and Skills

Tickell, Clare (March 2011) **The Early Years: Foundations for life, health and learning** – An Independent Report on the Early Years Foundation Stage to Her Majesty's Government

Department for Education (March 2012) **Statutory Framework for the Early Years Foundation Stage** – Setting the standards for learning, development and care for children from birth to five

Characteristics of Effective Learning

There are a number of learning characteristics which are evident in all seven areas of learning and development (p.7, 2012). These are not sequential, and it is not possible to identify particular ages or stages when they may be achieved. Learning characteristics include:

- **Playing and exploring** – engagement

- **Active learning** – motivation

- **Creating and thinking critically** – thinking

These learning characteristics should not be considered as an outcome which is summative, or marked in a 'tick list' manner. They represent processes, and may be observed during formative assessment.

Observation

It is crucial to observe children during their participation in these activities in order to assess whether they are working at an appropriate level and to work out their next steps in learning. The differentiation planned in the activity provides suitable challenge for all children.

Children can behave very differently during group, guided, independent and one-to-one opportunities. Some may be very quiet, and appear withdrawn or insecure during a group activity. However, given the opportunity to work with a close friend independently or at a self-chosen activity, a far more confident child may become apparent. Regular observation should therefore be a central part of good early years practice, ensuring that children are observed during different types of activity (guided, shared, self-chosen or independent), in differently sized groups with a range of children and at different times of day.

Sometimes it is useful to have a focus for observation such as an area of development or to discover the style of a child's learning, but at other times it is just as useful to observe the child for a period of time simply to discover what they are all about. If it appears that the child is making good progress, and is able to achieve what is required in an activity it is important to be aware of their next steps in learning. By always providing an opportunity for children to extend their learning they will continue to be interested and motivated, enjoying learning and finding out about new ideas. All of these are valuable personal characteristics which will be necessary throughout the whole of a child's life.

Assessment

The new EYFS will expect practicioners to make judgements as to whether a child is meeting, exceeding or emerging in relation to the Early Learning Goals (ELGs). In addition to their judgements, practicioners will need to make an assessment against the 3 characterisitcs of effective learning (see Observation record sheet page 57). As previously discussed, a child's learning characteristics are not suitable for summative assessment in a 'can they/can't they' manner. Rather, they should be thought of as part of a child's learning journey. It is for this reason that I am not recommending the use of a 'tick list' to record achievement of each learning characteristic. However, a simple observation record could include the characteristics observed during the observation and the context. This would build into a collection of evidence showing each child's strengths and areas for development. An example of an individual observation record of learning characteristics is provided on page 57.

The ELGs in both the prime and specific areas of learning are set at the expected level for a child nearing the end of FS2. Some children may be working towards achieving these goals and some may be exceeding them – it is the nature of any cohort of children. Indeed, there is likely to be discrepancy at times in a child's attainment towards the ELGs between areas of learning – a child rarely makes equal and comparative progress in all areas across a period of a year or more. It is not necessary to record in a numerical manner how a child achieves, but by highlighting the statement which most closely matches the attainment of the child, it is possible to identify their level of understanding and plan the next steps in progressing towards and exceeding the ELGs.

Using the group record sheets

The group record sheets on pages 58-61 can be used to show how a group of children are achieving at any one time – as a snapshot. It does not show progress over time or individual children's next steps but may be useful as a tool to show a co-ordinator or setting leader the strengths and areas for development of a cohort. It is not possible to fit all specific areas of learning onto one sheet so you may need to photocopy some back to back. There are a variety of record sheets here for both specific and prime areas of development. The group record sheet on page 58 for Communication and Language (prime) and Literacy (specific) also gives the opportunity to record achievement in all three areas on the same sheet, as some activities use ELGs from all of these areas. You may choose to use a traffic light system to record where children are in relation to each area of learning.

Preparing to set sail

What shall we take

The children will be packing a tablecloth to take on our journey – can they remember everything that is packed?

Resources

★ Large checked tablecloth or tartan rug

★ Cane, stick or wooden walking stick

★ Cord or rope

★ Objects for a sea journey: binoculars, spare clothes, food and drink, sun hat, map, coins, teddy bear

★ Squares of fabric about 30 cm x 30 cm

★ Small pieces of paper

Storybooks

★ *Paddington* by Michael Bond

★ *Dick Whittington* (versions by Ladybird or Oxford Reading Tree)

Key vocabulary

- journey
- pack
- case
- bundle
- cloth
- binoculars
- telescope
- map
- chart
- belongings

Observation and assessment

Communication and Language	Expected statements (ELGs)
Listening and attention	Children listen attentively in a range of situations. They listen to stories, accurately anticipating key events and respond to what they hear with relevant comments, questions or actions.
Understanding	Children follow instructions involving several ideas or actions.

Literacy	Expected statements (ELGs)
Writing	Children use their phonic knowledge to write words in ways which match their spoken sounds. They also write some irregular common words. They write simple sentences which can be read by themselves and others. Some words are spelt correctly and others are phonetically plausible.

What to do

Explain to the children that they are going to pack up some things to take on a journey to sea. Read a Paddington story, and talk about how he had a suitcase with all of his belongings in it – look at the items he chose to bring over from Peru.

Show the children a picture of a cloth tied in a bundle to a stick (for example, as we see in stories such as Dick Whittington). Tell them that this is a traditional way of carrying belongings and that this is what pirates would have used, not a brand new suitcase. Spread out a piece of cloth or a rug on the floor and sit the children around the edge. Discuss together the types of things that would be needed on a long journey. Try to have anticipated what the children will suggest and have the items behind you to produce and lay on the cloth. If they suggest something that you do not have, write it on a flipchart to find later. Show the children how to bundle up the cloth and tie it to the stick.

Introduce the key vocabulary, ensuring that the children know the names of the items on the cloth. Encourage them to point to each item and say the name.

Play a simple memory game: cover all the items on the floor with the cloth and ask the children to recall all the items underneath, how many can they remember? They could work with a partner to see if they can name them all, or work as a whole group, each naming an item for the adult to pull out from under the cloth.

If this is to be a guided activity…

…then the children can work together with an adult to create their own bundle using a square of fabric and pictures of objects they could take. Encourage them to draw a simple picture of each item they would pack, and attempt to label it using phonetically plausible spelling. Put the pictures together on the square of cloth and tie together to a stick.

If this is to be an independent activity…

…then show the children where the collection of objects to take on a journey is and provide a large cloth. Let the children work with a partner or in a small group to lay out some of the objects on the floor and then cover them up to play the memory game. Provide small whiteboards for the children to make a list of the hidden items, either pictorially or with emergent writing.

To support or extend

To support, put out a simple selection of objects with initial phonemes that the children already know or are easy to spell, for example: hat, ted, cup, map, mat. Take turns in asking the children to put one of the objects at a time onto the cloth to ensure that they know what it is called. The adult could differentiate the questioning where appropriate, e.g. 'Evie please put something beginning with 't' onto the cloth', 'Poppy, can you pack something that sounds the same as 'mat'?' The adult could scribe each item onto a flipchart, sounding out as they write.

To extend, tell the children that they can take only items beginning with a particular phoneme, an item beginning with each letter of the alphabet or containing a certain long vowel phoneme. To begin, play a game in a small group along the lines of, 'I went to sea and I took with me…an apple. I went to sea and I took with me…a banana.' The children could then attempt to record some of these items by drawing little pictures on sticky notes to attach to a flipchart, putting them in alphabetical order.

Ideas for interactive display

Display the alphabet on the wall. Have large pieces of paper cut into the shape of checked cloth bundles labelled with a letter of the alphabet. These could be in alphabetical order or labelled with letters corresponding to phases from Letters and Sounds, for example Phase Two: satpin. Provide objects for the children to 'pack' by placing them on the relevant letter of the alphabet.

Parents and carers as partners

At home, talk together about what to pack for an outing. If going for a walk or to visit a friend encourage your child to consider what they could put in their bag – for example a drink, a snack, something to colour or play with, a hat or gloves. Talk about the purpose of the excursion and what they will need on different outings.

Preparing to set sail

Maps and routes

The children will be using positional and directional language in making and reading a map, firstly in the small world and then onto paper. Using creasing, tearing and staining with cold teabags to make the maps look old.

Observation and assessment

Mathematics	Expected statements (ELGs)
Shape, space and measures	Children use everyday language to talk about size, weight, capacity, position, distance, time and money to compare quantities and objects and to solve problems. They recognise, create and describe patterns. They explore characteristics of everyday objects and shapes and use mathematical language to describe them.

Key vocabulary

• position	• sand	• rocks
• in front	• shore	• environment
• behind	• trees	• near
• next to	• forest	• far
• between	• mountain	• furthest
• island	• beach	• nearest
• sea	• fields	

Resources

★ Simple maps as examples (from parks, playgrounds and animal farms with colour and symbols)

★ White paper

★ Cold, used teabags

★ Matches (adult use)

★ Ribbon cut into short lengths

★ Sand tray or tuff spot

★ Natural materials (moss, pine cones, pebbles, sand)

★ Small world people and animals

Safety first!

Matches are for adult use only, to be kept safely out of reach. Ensure matches are cool before disposing of them.

Storybooks and non-fiction books

★ *As the Crow Flies: A First Book of Maps* by Gail Hartman

★ *Katie Morag Delivers the Mail* by Mairi Hedderwick (and others in the series, each has a simple map sketched in the cover)

★ *Winnie the Pooh books* by A.A. Milne (a map of the Hundred Acre Wood sketched inside the cover)

What to do

Explain to the children that they are going to build a small world environment in the sand tray that might be similar to somewhere they could discover on their sea journey. Talk about going on a journey and looking over the sea from the edge of their boat: imagine what they would see. Act it out together and practise shouting 'Land ahoy!' Ask each child what they can see: trees! Are they tall or short? Ask another child what they can see: – mountains! What shape are they? Are they in front of or behind the trees? Continue for several more children, using positional language each time to build up a virtual landscape.

Discuss the environment they have imagined, and explain that they are going to create it now as a group in the sand tray or tuff spot. Sit the children around the edge, and show them the materials and objects gathered together for this activity. Select the same children who shared their ideas before to come out and create their view, e.g. 'Let's put your trees onto our land Joe – what shall we use? Can you see anything the correct shape? Now George let's add your mountains – were they in front or behind the trees?' Introduce the key mathematical vocabulary during the discussion. Encourage all the children to take part by opening the questioning to others, asking them to confirm what the original children said.

When the 'land' is complete with several easy to draw features, explain to the children that they are going to make a picture of their land, or a 'map', to remember where everything is. Demonstrate drawing some of the features on a flipchart, speaking out loud and using the positional language when adding each feature. Let the children use small world people or animals to play in the environment you have created together.

If this is to be a guided activity...

...then the children can work together in a small group with an adult to create a physical island environment. Talk about likely natural features that would be seen and encourage the children to add these in appropriate places, e.g. a beach next to the sea. Give the children a piece of paper and let them draw their created land onto it, using pictures and symbols to illustrate the features. Frequently stop the children and question them about their map using positional language, e.g. 'So you have put the trees between the rocks and the beach?' Show them how to tear the edges of their paper to make it look old, scrunch it up to add creases and finally rub a cold wet teabag over it to make the paper look aged. An adult could use matches to scorch the edge of the paper to add further effect.

If this is to be an independent activity...

...then show the children where the box of resources will be, and explain that they can try this activity sometime this week. Let them work in small groups to create a physical environment from the natural materials provided. Show them how to age the paper by tearing, scrunching, creasing, folding and staining. Provide crayons, differently sized, shaped and coloured paper and cold teabags or watery coffee and brushes for staining the paper after they have made their maps. Let them roll up their maps and use pieces of ribbon to tie them into a scroll shape.

To support or extend

To support, make some word cards with positional language on, e.g. in front of, behind, next to, between. Using the physical island created from natural materials play a question and answer game with a few children. Put the cards face down in a pile. As the adult selects one and shows the children they say the word together. Demonstrate using the word in a sentence appropriately, e.g. 'Between: The mountain is between the sea and the forest.' Encourage the children to then use the same word in a sentence of their own, looking at their physical land for ideas.

To extend, use string to create a simple coordinates grid over the physical map, and help the children to draw vertical and horizontal lines over their written map. Show them how to label the squares in a simple grid A, B, C/1, 2, 3 and use the references to ask them about the location of their map features. They could draw a feature on a sticky note and write the coordinate on the back, to play a guessing game with their friend.

Ideas for interactive display

- Provide an area for the physical map to be displayed in its tray. Put out other items and objects around the edge for other children to use to add to the virtual world. Include simple word cards with the positional language for the children to read and begin to recognise.

- Have multiple copies of maps showing places the children know well, for example a local park, high street or even the school. Let them use these to ask each other questions – can you see the church? How many swings are there? Which way would you walk to get to the pond?

Parents and carers as partners

At home or when out and about look at maps and plans in the local environment. Supermarkets often have simple maps of the stores, and parks sometimes have maps to show where the car park or toilets are. Stop to look at these when you are with your child, and locate the 'You are here!' arrow. Can your child find another place on the map?

Preparing to set sail

Let's build a boat

The children will be creating a large-scale role-play by building a boat, using large-scale construction including planks, crates, ropes and cloth tarpaulins. They can walk the plank and have water thrown at them!

Observation and assessment

Understanding the world	Expected statements (ELGs)
The world	Children know about similarities and differences in relation to places, objects, materials and living things. They make observations of animals and plants and explain why some things occur, and talk about changes.

Resources

★ Large planks, beams, blocks, bread trays, milk crates, boxes, ropes, sheets, tarpaulin (or car covers)

★ Pictures of different types of boats and ships either printed or on the whiteboard

★ Water pistols with water in

★ Blue tissue paper

★ Large pieces of blue fabric or sheets

★ Clipboards and pencils

★ Hard hats/high visibility vests/role-play clothing to dress up as 'builders'

★ Digital camera

Storybooks and non-fiction books

★ *Busy Boats (Amazing Machines)* by Tony Mitton

★ *All Afloat on Noah's Boat* by Tony Mitton

★ *The Boy Who Built the Boat* by Ross Mueller

Key vocabulary

- boat
- ship
- deck
- cabin
- bow
- prow
- sail
- anchor
- chain
- portholes
- ladders
- steps
- wood
- plank
- beam
- box
- crate
- rope
- tarpaulin
- sheet

What to do

Explain to the children that they are going to build a boat together using large objects such as planks and crates. Look at some pictures of boats and discuss the common features between them, they have a deck, cabin, bow, sail, anchor, portholes and so on. Talk about the purposes of each of these features, introducing the key vocabulary. Ask the children simple questions to check that they understand the words used and can identify the features of a boat. Discuss the practicalities of a boat – how do the people climb aboard onto the boat? Where do they sit? Where can they eat or sleep? What is the anchor for? How is it lowered over the side? Encourage all children to join in with the discussion, assessing their understanding by listening to their questions and responses when they chat with their friends.

Show the children the selection of large objects that you have gathered together for them to build with. Before they begin to build, sit in a circle around the objects on the floor and remind the children of the key features of a boat. What is the deck for? Can you see anything here that would be useful in creating a deck? What could we make an anchor from? How would we climb aboard the boat?

Allow the children to work together in small groups initially, investigating the objects and creating their boats. Use the digital camera to record the boats as they are built, reviewed and changed.

Let the children lay down the blue plastic sheeting to represent the sea around the boat and add a plank. Allow the other children to squirt them with water pistols or throw dry blue tissue paper streamers at them as they 'walk the plank' and fall into the 'sea'.

If this is to be a guided activity…

…then the children can work together with an adult to create a boat. Look together at the pictures of boats and choose several features which your boat will have, e.g. a deck, a bow and a ramp for boarding. Help the children to select appropriate objects to create the features. Challenge them by asking if they can choose a wider ramp or create a flatter deck. Let them amend their structure as they build, reviewing and changing as they work. Take photographs of the boat for the children to show the class later, so that they can answer questions from the rest of the group.

If this is to be an independent activity…

…then show the children where the selection of objects are and explain that they can try this activity sometime this week. Provide role-play clothes such as hard hats and high visibility waistcoats for the children to wear whilst building. Encourage them to use the correct vocabulary when they are designing and building, and to regularly check their own progress and amend the build if necessary. If possible, leave the 'boat' out at the end of each session so that different children can add to it or make changes to the original design. Photograph it at different stages each day.

To support or extend

To support, help the children to create a simple container boat big enough to fit inside a couple of children and some toy animals. Read or tell the story of Noah (such as All Afloat on Noah's Boat), and how he built a boat large enough to carry two of every kind of animal in the world. Talk with the children about the best objects available to create a boat shape, and support them in creating this. For example, put out a mat and let the children lay blocks around the edges, or use large sheets and cloths to create 'sea'.

To extend, encourage the children to design their boat before building it: help them to draw a simple plan on a clipboard and label the main features of the boat using the correct key vocabulary. Share each other's plans in a small group before building any of them – which aspects do the children think will work well? Are there any which may not work at all? Why not? Use the plans when building and take photographs to show the children afterwards – did they follow their plans? Why? What changes did they make, if any? If they were to build a boat again what would they do differently?

Ideas for interactive display

- Provide an area with different pictures of boats, clearly labelled with the key vocabulary. Put out small construction equipment such as Lego or wooden bricks for the children to use to build boats or ships of their own.

- Display the photographs taken by the children of their large-scale boat building. Let them talk about the most successful, and provide a clipboard for a 'shopping wish list' for next time a similar activity is planned – encourage the children to write or draw objects they would find useful next time.

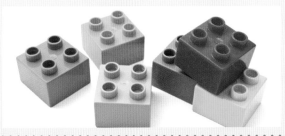

Parents and carers as partners

At home, use everyday objects to make boats, homes and dens. Items such as chairs, clothes airers, fireguards, sofa cushions, towels, blankets and clothes pegs all combine to make great hiding spaces for children to crawl into and take a favourite teddy, book or a picnic snack. No special equipment is needed, and the best thing is that it is all taken down at the end of the day, to be rebuilt differently tomorrow.

Preparing to set sail

Printing 'great waves'

The children will be looking at Hokusai's 'The Great Wave of Kanagawa' pictures, and printing their own versions.

Observation and assessment

Expressive arts and design	Expected statements (ELGs)
Exploring and using media and materials	They safely use and explore a variety of materials, tools and techniques, experimenting with colour, design, texture, form and function.
Being imaginative	Children use what they have learnt about media and materials in original ways, thinking about uses and purposes. They represent their own ideas, thoughts and feelings through design and technology, art, music, dance, role-play and stories.

Key vocabulary

- print
- paint
- press
- smooth
- roll
- engrave
- carve
- wood
- woodcut

Resources

- ★ Printing ink and thick paint
- ★ Polystyrene sheets
- ★ Rollers or a rolling pin or sponge pieces
- ★ Differently sized, shaped and coloured pieces of paper
- ★ Potatoes and a sharp knife (for adult use only)
- ★ Large pieces of paper
- ★ Card folded to make greeting cards
- ★ Viewfinders (made from pieces of card with the centre cut out)
- ★ Balls, marbles and objects that roll
- ★ Curved objects such as construction equipment, disposable cups etc.
- ★ Roll of lining paper
- ★ Small trays with sides
- ★ Paper cut to the size of the trays

Storybooks and non-fiction books

- ★ *Wave* by Suzy Lee
- ★ *Mrs Armitage and the Big Wave* by Quentin Blake
- ★ *The Old Man Mad About Drawing – A Tale Of Hokusai* by Francois Place
- ★ *The Great Wave: A Children's Book Inspired by Hokusai* by Veronique Massenot
- ★ *One Day in Japan With Hokusai (Adventures in Art)* by Julia Altmann

What to do

Explain to the children that they are going to look at some different books with pictures of waves in them, and have a go at printing some wave pictures of their own. Read the picture books *Wave* and *Mrs Armitage and the Big Wave* and discuss the illustrations with the children. What do they think about the waves in the stories? Can they use some words to describe them? Look at how the artists (Suzy Lee and Quentin Blake) have drawn the waves. Talk about the shapes and colours used.

Introduce the work of the artist Hokusai and show the children some of his prints. Explain that these were created differently from the illustrations in the storybooks as they are woodcut prints and not drawings. Introduce the key vocabulary when describing how the prints were made. Demonstrate, using the polystyrene sheets (cut into smaller tiles approximately 10 cm x 10 cm), drawing a simple wave in the style of the swirly wave motif from Hokusai onto the tile with a pencil or biro. Ensure that the shape is pressed into the polystyrene but has not punctured it. Roll some ink onto the roller in a small tray and roll it onto the tile. Alternatively use a sponge to dab thick paint onto the tile. Press the tile onto the paper, showing the children how to gently peel it off without smudging the print. Repeat this action a few more times at the side of the first print, commenting how the image becomes fainter each time.

If this is to be a guided activity…

…then the children can work together in a group with an adult to make their own print from a tile. Practise drawing wavy motifs on whiteboards first until the children are happy with their design. Draw the wave shape onto the small tile and help them to make prints. They look attractive on A4 sized paper in a two by two pattern. To make the print more colourful use more than one colour of paint when printing – put a dab of blue, green and white onto the roller before covering the tile with paint.

If this is to be an independent activity…

…then show the children where the box of art resources will be, and explain that they can try this activity sometime this week. Provide lots of objects with curved edges for the children to print with, e.g. disposable cups and bowls cut in half, pieces of construction equipment or train track, corks and pieces of foil to fold and bend. Explain to the children that they can use any of the objects to print with, overlapping and repeating the curves in different sizes and colours until the picture has built up into a sea full of waves. Roll out a large sheet of lining paper outdoors for the children to make their own 'Great Wave' by rolling and printing with different objects.

To support or extend

To support, put a sheet of clean paper in a tray and squirt a blob of blue paint at the end. Put a marble into the tray and show the children how to gently tip the tray so that the marble rolls through the paint and around the tray, making wavy tracks as it goes. Can the children make it roll from end to end, or make wavy tracks along the paper? Put in another blob of paint of a different colour such as white and watch as the tracks overlap or swirl together. To make a shimmery effect, sprinkle white or silver glitter onto the paint tracks before they dry.

To extend, look carefully at the foam swirls at the end of Hokusai's waves. Talk about the shapes and colours used, and explain to the children that they are going to make a small card with a print of this. Focus on the smallest details in the wave crest (using a viewfinder: a small piece of card with a hole cut in it to help them to study a small area) and practise on whiteboards first. Use a felt pen to draw on a potato cut in half, drying it with a paper towel. Let the adult carve out the design with a sharp knife, and let the children make prints onto cards to send to their friends or family.

Ideas for interactive display

- Provide an area for display of many different pictures of waves, including those by Hokusai. Laminate some on postcard shapes and let the children sort and display them by pegging them onto a washing line – these all have one boat in them; these have more than six people.

- Encourage the children to bring in any photographs they have at home or any pictures from magazines showing waves or the sea. Display these all together to create a collage – perhaps displaying them in colour shade order, from deep blue to light blue.

Parents and carers as partners

At home, do some simple potato printing on large pieces of paper such as old wallpaper or flattened cardboard boxes. Cut a large potato in half and press a pastry cutter into one of the cut sides. Using this as a guide, cut away about 2 cm of the potato around the edges of the cutter, leaving a raised shape. Press this raised shape into paint and use it to print with. Make repeating patterns or stamp the letters in your child's name. Printing a festive shape like a star or a tree onto lining paper can make large sheets of Christmas wrapping paper!

Climb aboard

Telescopes: 'I see a...'

The children will be making and using a telescope to say and write simple sentences, beginning with 'I see a…'

Resources

★ Telescope and binoculars

★ Cardboard tubes

★ Gold or silver paper

★ Craft materials

★ Masking tape

★ Hole punch

★ String

★ Small whiteboards and pens

★ Speech bubble shapes, made from white paper and laminated

★ Dry wipe pens

Storybooks

★ *Sophie and the Seagull* by Petra Engels-Fietzek

★ *Brown Bear, Brown Bear, What Do You See?* by Bill Martin Jnr

Observation and assessment

Communication and Language	Expected statements (ELGs)
Listening and attention	Children listen attentively in a range of situations.
Speaking	Children express themselves effectively, showing awareness of listeners' needs. They use past, present and future forms accurately when talking about events that have happened or are to happen in the future.

Literacy	Expected statements (ELGs)
Writing	Children use their phonic knowledge to write words in ways which match their spoken sounds. They also write some irregular common words. They write simple sentences which can be read by themselves and others. Some words are spelt correctly and others are phonetically plausible.

Key vocabulary

- telescope
- binoculars
- see
- look
- view
- crow's nest
- repeated sentences beginning with 'I see a…'
- speech bubbles

What to do

Read the book *Sophie's Seagull* and talk about her telescope. If possible, have an actual telescope or binoculars for the children to look at and pass around. Explain that a telescope helps you to see things far away, and that on a boat journey the sailors would climb up high (often to a place called the 'crow's nest' – explain why this would be a suitable name) and use a telescope to look at what they could see far away. Use the key vocabulary in the discussion. Introduce the book *Brown Bear, Brown Bear, What Do You See?* and ask the children to join in with you and say the repeated refrain 'I see a…'

Discuss what a sailor or pirate may see from the crow's nest and write a list on the flipchart from the children's suggestions. Show the children the laminated speech bubbles and demonstrate writing 'I see a tree' on it with a dry wipe pen. Encourage the children to work independently to write their own simple sentence on a speech bubble using phonics and phonetically plausible attempts at words.

In the guided activity following, the children can make a telescope from a cardboard tube and attach a picture of the object they can see to display alongside their speech bubble.

If this is to be a guided activity…

…then the children can work together with an adult to make a telescope from a cardboard tube. They can use craft materials to decorate it however they wish, and add gold or silver strips of paper around the tube to look like metal bands. Draw around the end of the tube on a piece of white paper and draw an object inside the circle. Colour and cut it out, and let the adult laminate it. This picture can be attached to the end of the tube with sticky tape and it will look like it is 'in view' when the telescope is used.

If this is to be an independent activity…

…then show the children where the collection of box model tubes, cylinders and cardboard is and explain to the children that they are to make either a telescope or a pair of binoculars independently. Provide masking tape for joining as it is easy for children to tear and it can be painted over, and a hole punch and string for them to attach string so that they can be worn around their necks. Let them practise measuring the tubes to the appropriate length. An adult may be needed to help cut them.

To support or extend

To support, help the children to make a sentence to go on the speech bubble. Reread the book *Brown Bear, Brown Bear* together, ensuring that they can say a sentence in the style of 'Brown Bear, Brown Bear'. Write the words 'I see a' onto three individual word cards, and let them choose an animal to 'see'. Write this animal on a sticky note or have a small picture for the children to use. Help them to put the words in the correct order to build the sentence. These can be Blu tacked onto the speech bubble.

To extend, consider the other senses and help the children to write more simple sentences such as 'I hear a…' or 'I smell a…'. Ask the children to think of a specific environment such as a desert or a jungle, and to try to only consider creatures or environmental features from these places.

Ideas for interactive display

- Put some familiar classroom objects on a display table. Take some extreme close up photographs of parts of these objects, for example the hole in a pencil sharpener; the end of a pencil; one key from a mobile phone or calculator. Encourage the children to match the photographs to the objects.

- Provide a selection of magnifying glasses, lenses, old glasses, binoculars and telescopes for the children to investigate.

- If you have a microscope or digital microscope which can be plugged in to display on a computer screen show the children how to put things underneath it and view them.

Parents and carers as partners

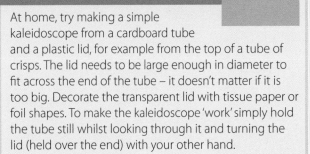

At home, try making a simple kaleidoscope from a cardboard tube and a plastic lid, for example from the top of a tube of crisps. The lid needs to be large enough in diameter to fit across the end of the tube – it doesn't matter if it is too big. Decorate the transparent lid with tissue paper or foil shapes. To make the kaleidoscope 'work' simply hold the tube still whilst looking through it and turning the lid (held over the end) with your other hand.

Climb aboard

Designing and making a flag

The children will be investigating patterns by using three colours to design a coloured flag, and investigating how many different ways there are to colour it.

Resources

★ Coloured beanbags, Unifix cubes and crayons in three different colours

★ Large rectangle divided into three equal sections, such as the French or Italian flag

★ Three differently coloured pieces of paper, each as big as one of the sections on the large blank flag

★ Smaller pieces of paper with a rectangular flag divided into three equal sections on it (like a blank version of the French or Italian flag)

★ Blu tack

★ Squared paper

★ Lolly sticks

★ Digital camera

Storybooks

★ *Sail Away, Little Boat* by Janet Buell

★ *Sail Away* by Florence McNeil

Key vocabulary

• colour	• third	• last
• pattern	• stripe	• top
• half	• first	• middle
• quarter	• next	• bottom

Observation and assessment

Mathematics	Expected statements (ELGs)
Numbers	Children count reliably with numbers from 1 to 20, place them in order and say which number is one more or one less than a given number. They solve problems, including doubling, halving and sharing.

Mathematics	Expected statements (ELGs)
Shape, space and measures	Children use everyday language to talk about size, weight, capacity, position, distance, time and money to compare quantities and objects and to solve problems. They recognise, create and describe patterns. They explore characteristics of everyday objects and shapes and use mathematical language to describe them.

What to do

Explain to the children that they are going to design a flag for the ship, but that they only have three colours of material. Show them the beanbags, let them pass them around. Talk about how they are all of equal size, and that they can be placed next to each other in a pattern. As a starter activity, give out all the beanbags and ask the children to put themselves into threes with children holding differently coloured beanbags. (If your group number is not divisible by three, pair some children to share a bean bag). Check the groupings – each group of three children should have three differently coloured beanbags. Choose a group and ask them to stand together in a line – which colour is first? Which is in the middle? At the end? Ask the other children to make a line with the colours in a different order. Discuss together how there are still three colours but that the order has changed. Show the children the flipchart flag, and put the coloured pieces of paper on the flag with Blu-tack. Introduce the key vocabulary, explaining that the flag is divided into three sections and that these are called 'thirds'. Explain that there are six different ways to place the three colours to make a flag. Encourage the children to colour the small paper flags with the three differently coloured crayons to show their ideas. Attach lolly sticks down one side of the paper as a flagpole to distinguish the top of the flag from the bottom so that they are not placed upside down. Let the children work with a partner or two to put their ideas together. If each pair or group has a large piece of paper they can lay out their coloured flags looking for patterns or any methods they have missed.

If this is to be a guided activity…

…then the children can work together with an adult to create and record as many different ways of making a coloured flag using only three colours. Put out the coloured Unifix cubes and let the children build towers to show the six different ways of placing the three colours. When they have built all six give them some squared paper and ask them to record by colouring the different patterns they have. Try to encourage them to be systematic in their investigations and to record accurately. Ask them to explain to you how they went about finding all the options.

If this is to be an independent activity…

…then show the children where the box of resources will be, and explain that they can try this activity sometime this week. Provide a mixture of resources in the three colours, e.g. red, blue and green. Include bricks, beads and strings, threading cotton reels, peg and pegboards, coloured construction, crayons, paint and printing sponges and toy cars or train carriages and track. Explain to them that they are to use whichever medium they prefer to investigate the placing of the three colours. Provide a digital camera for them to record their findings.

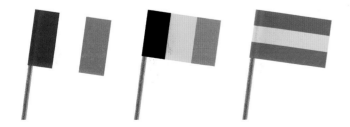

To support or extend

To support, give each child a red, green and blue brick. Ask them to make a tower, and then compare their tower with that of a partner. If they are the same pattern then take the towers apart and try again; if they are different then keep them on the table and make some more. Keep going until the children feel they have exhausted all the options. Use the vocabulary top, middle, bottom, first, next, and last, until the children are familiar with it.

To extend, allow the children to still use the three colours but explain that the flag does not have to use each of the colours every time, for example each of the three sections could be coloured red, or two red and one blue, or one red, one blue and one green. Try to show the children how to be systematic in their investigations, taking one colour at a time and adding other colours to it. Record by colouring in small flags on paper, or by using squared paper to draw and colour the flags.

Ideas for interactive display

- Put the photographs from the independent activity out on a table – can the other children replicate the pattern made on a bead string on the track using train carriages?

- Have a washing line with differently coloured pegs and coloured socks on it. Let the children investigate pattern making – can their friend continue a pattern they have started? Encourage them to complicate their patterns – use differently coloured pegs; hang some of the socks upside down!

- Display the flags of the countries of the world and look at the colours and symbols used. Provide some paper and lolly sticks for the children to design and colour their own flag.

Parents and carers as partners

At home, use differently coloured buttons, stones, beads or sweets to make patterns. Begin with a two colour repeating pattern, e.g. red/blue/red/blue. Can your child continue a pattern you have started? Can they make one for you to continue? The patterns can be as complicated or as simple as is necessary. If the objects vary in size and shape as well as colour the patterns can become quite complicated, e.g. two small blue/one big red/a green/two small blue etc. Be inventive where you leave patterns for your child – with their bricks on the edge of the bath; on their plate with peas, ketchup and sweetcorn; on their bed in coloured socks; at the park or on the beach with natural materials such as leaves, sticks, cones and shells.

Climb aboard

Will it float or sink?

The children will be using the water tray to investigate how much cargo a boat can carry before sinking.

Resources

* ★ Plastic duck bath toy

* ★ Bucketful of washed pea gravel

* ★ Some boats of identical size and weight with room to carry some pea gravel or some shallow plastic containers to act as boats

* ★ String

* ★ Large water tray

* ★ Weighing scales

* ★ Two sorting hoops

* ★ Selection of familiar items for the children to investigate whether they float or sink: pencil, metal pencil sharpener, metal fork, plastic medicine spoon, paper clip, coin, marble, wooden clothes peg

Storybooks

* ★ *Ten Little Rubber Ducks* by Eric Carle

* ★ *Who Sank the Boat?* by Pamela Allen

Observation and assessment

Understanding the world	Expected statements (ELGs)
The world	Children know about similarities and differences in relation to places, objects, materials and living things. They make observations of animals and plants and explain why some things occur, and talk about changes.
Technology	Children recognise that a range of technology is used in places such as homes and schools. They select and use technology for particular purposes.

Key vocabulary

* float
* sink
* flood
* fill
* heavy
* light
* more
* less
* long
* short
* fat
* thin
* wide
* narrow
* even
* equal
* cargo
* container ship
* overboard

What to do

Read the story *Ten Little Rubber Ducks* to the children and show them the duck bath toy. Explain that the story was written after a large container ship carrying millions of little plastic ducks lost its cargo overboard. As the little ducks were made from plastic they floated over the ocean to different countries and beaches everywhere, and that they never made it to their intended destination. Explain to the children that they are going to be the captain of a boat with a very important cargo. They are to carry some rocks over to an island to help build a new castle. Show them the small pebbles (pea gravel is very good for this as the pebbles are roughly the same size and will fit inside a small boat). Tell them that the King of the island is going to give a reward to the team of children that can take the most gravel across in one load without sinking. Show the children the toy boats or shallow plastic containers that you are to use as boats. Explain that there are different ways to fill the boat: pile the load up at one end; make two piles at the front and the back; spread the stones evenly around the boat. Demonstrate different methods, predicting and reviewing what happens. Discuss the best way to pull the boat across the water tray with the string – gently, jerkily or suddenly? Slowly or quickly? Introduce the key vocabulary, ensuring that the children know what the words mean and can use them correctly. Demonstrate counting the stones into the boat at the beginning of the journey and out at the other end if the journey was successful. Record each score after each attempt. Reward the winning boat captains with chocolate gold coins!

If this is to be a guided activity…

…then the children can work together with an adult to predict which method will be most successful and give reasons for their choices. Use the flipchart to draw the different options of carrying the cargo in the boat – in a heap at one end, at the sides or evenly spread. Let the children choose which picture they wish to vote for. Let the children test out their theories, and change their vote if they feel it necessary. Investigate different sizes, shapes and amounts of pebbles and gravel, listening carefully to the language the children are using. Consolidate their knowledge by careful questioning.

If this is to be an independent activity…

…then show the children where the basket of resources is and explain that they can try this activity sometime this week. Provide a selection of natural materials that are different sizes and have different properties, e.g. pine cones, stones, sticks (long and short), moss, flowers and feathers. Let the children work together to fill the 'boats' and pull them across the water tray without losing any cargo. Encourage them to record their findings pictorially as 'emergent mathematics'.

To support or extend

To support, have a selection of familiar items for the children to investigate whether they float or sink. For example: pencil, metal pencil sharpener, metal fork, plastic medicine spoon, paper clip, coin, marble, wooden clothes peg, cork, lid from a bottle. Put out the two sorting hoops and ask the children to put the objects into groups of those they think will float and those they think won't. Let them test them in the water, and put them into the correct hoop. Were they accurate in their predictions? Draw the children's attention to the materials the objects are made from – does that make a difference? What is similar about the floating objects?

To extend, have a selection of pebbles, stones and gravel of different sizes and explain to the children that they are going to use the weighing scales to predict which cargo will float and which will sink. Select a medium-sized pebble which floats in the boat, and show the children how to weigh it on the scales.

Put a sticker on the scales to show the weight. Explain that any cargo lighter than the pebble should float. Demonstrate putting small pieces of gravel onto the scales until the weight is the same as that of the pebble. Put the gravel cargo into the boat – does it float? Investigate with differently sized stones and pebbles, encouraging the children to compare size and weight and make predictions when estimating.

Ideas for interactive display

- Put the small objects to be tested out on the display table, with a shallow tray of water for the children to test whether they float or sink. Include some objects which can be counted and measured, for example, if one pencil floats, will two taped together? What about more than one cork taped together? If an empty lid floats will it still float with a little water inside?

- On the wall display many different pictures of different water craft. Include huge tankers, passenger ferries, one man kayaks and jet skis. Leave room for the children to draw and add more of their own.

Safety first!

Never leave a child to play in the bath unattended – they can drown in as little as an inch of water.

Parents and carers as partners

At home, play in the bath with your child, filling differently sized containers with items such as marbles. Take it in turns to put a marble in the 'boat', counting each one – who will sink the boat?

Climb aboard

Star constellations

The children will be looking at star constellations and making pictures and patterns of their own using black paper punched with holes.

Resources

- ★ Computer with internet connection

- ★ Black card and paper cut into approximately A5/A4 sizes

- ★ Modelling clay

- ★ Sharp pencils

- ★ White pencil crayons

- ★ Silver star stickers

- ★ White finger paint

- ★ Matchsticks

- ★ Compass to show north, south, east and west

- ★ Overhead projector with a flat glass horizontal top

- ★ Pale ceiling or screen

- ★ Selection of objects with holes or spaces in: pencil sharpener, sieve, potato masher, fork, key, beads or pasta, construction toys, scissors

- ★ Hole punch

Storybooks and non-fiction books

- ★ *Little Bear, You're a Star!: A Greek Myth About the Constellations* by Jean Marzollo

- ★ *Stars! Stars! Stars!* by Nancy Elizabeth Wallace

- ★ *The Biggest Bear* by Adam Relf

Observation and assessment

Expressive arts and design	Expected statements (ELGs)
Exploring and using media and materials	They safely use and explore a variety of materials, tools and techniques, experimenting with colour, design, texture, form and function.
Being imaginative	Children use what they have learnt about media and materials in original ways, thinking about uses and purposes.
	They represent their own ideas, thoughts and feelings through design and technology, art, music, dance, role-play and stories.

Key vocabulary

- • star
- • constellation
- • night
- • light
- • sky
- • dark

- • moon
- • light
- • map
- • plan
- • journey
- • direction

- • navigate
- • north
- • south
- • east
- • west

What to do

Read one or more of the books about stars and constellations. Look at a website showing star maps, and explain to the children that broadly speaking the same stars appear in the same place in the night sky at the same time each night. Look at some of the most familiar constellations which are easy to distinguish. Tell the children that many years ago people gave the groups of stars names, as they believed that they resembled creatures and objects. Show on the flipchart how they are similar to dot-to-dot pictures, made from lines and dots (stars) in key places.

Ask the children to close their eyes, and imagine they are sailing on a ship in the middle of a huge ocean. The waves are going up and down, the boat is going up and down and it is night time. There is no land in sight at all; no lights, no houses, no trees, no other people or boats, and all that you can see is the night sky. It is full of stars and the moon. Explain that the only way you will know which direction to travel in is to use the stars to guide you.

Discuss how the sailors could do this – talk about the directions of north, south, east and west and let the children look at the compass. Introduce the key vocabulary, explaining how the sailors would have looked each night for the same star patterns in the sky and sailed towards them, using them like a map. Explain to the children that they are going to create their own star pattern (or constellation) and that it is going to be displayed onto the wall or ceiling as if it were actually made from stars.

If this is to be a guided activity...

...then the children can work together with an adult to draw a simple animal or creature shape onto black card, using a white crayon so it shows up. Let the children stick silver stars onto the key points of their drawing. With support, they can draw over the white lines with a silver pen or a correctional fluid tape dispenser, so that the picture can be seen by the rest of the children at a short distance.

With adult help, let them push the sharpened pencil point into the centre of each silver star to make a hole in the paper (put the modelling clay underneath). When all the stars have holes, display the picture to the rest of the class by laying it on an overhead projector to allow light through the holes onto the ceiling, creating a star pattern. Encourage the other children to guess what animal it may be. Show the picture to let them see if they were correct.

If this is to be an independent activity...

...then show the children where the box of resources will be, and explain that they can try this activity sometime this week. Provide an overhead projector and a selection of objects with holes or spaces in, for example pencil sharpener, sieve, potato masher, fork, key, beads or pasta, construction toys, scissors. Tape a cardboard screen around three sides of the projector so the children in the 'audience' cannot see what another child is placing on the projector glass. Arrange the projector so that the image is projected onto the ceiling – can the other children recognise the item? Try the same object from a variety of angles – are some images easier to discern than others?

To support or extend

To support, make star pictures using white finger paint onto black paper. Let the children print random white dots over all the paper. Then, join some of the dots together by laying the matchsticks on the paper. Can they make a square/a smile/a snake? When they have made an image they are pleased with show them how to draw with a white crayon in the place of the matchsticks, or glue them down. (Paper art straws work for this as well, but they need cutting into much smaller pieces, and children can become preoccupied with finding the piece of art straw that is exactly the correct length to join two dots, forgetting their original purpose).

To extend, allow the children to use hole punches (the single one handed ones with a longish reach, which look like nutcrackers are best for this) to create pictures of their own. Encourage them to draw capital letters, and place stars where there is a join of the lines or curves. Punch holes over these stars and place them on the overhead projector. Can their friends recognise the letters they have made?

Ideas for interactive display

- Put the pictures of constellations and star patterns on a display table, along with a torch. Let the children shine the torch through the holey paper – can they see the image?

- Provide a variety of other holey items for the children to shine the torch through, for example a piece of net curtain, lace, a cheese grater or a strainer. Investigate the patterns which can be made – do they change as the light source moves closer and further away? Pin large sheets of paper on the wall for the children to draw on the light and shadows created when the torch light passes through the holes in the grater.

Parents and carers as partners

At home, go out into the night sky and try to look for the moon and stars (the moon is sometimes visible in the daytime too). Talk about the patterns you can see, and the brightest or most twinkly stars. Let your child find something in the sky to show you. If you have a pair of binoculars your child may like to play with these, but a simple homemade cardboard tube 'telescope' will also let them focus on a smaller area of night sky. If it is the wrong time of year to catch the night sky (i.e. your child goes to bed before sundown) try looking on the internet at pictures of the night sky, or in a book from the library.

Safety first!

Remind your child never to look directly at the sun, as it will damage their eyes.

Pirates ahoy!

'Wanted' posters

The children will be making a 'wanted' poster for a pirate, drawing and adding labels to describe them.

Resources

★ Examples of posters showing information

★ Blank A4 poster outlines with a border and Wanted! written across the top

★ Pencils and crayons

★ Collage materials: wool, fabric triangles, black circles, string, gold/silver ribbon

★ Large colour pictures of faces cut from newspaper supplements and magazines

Storybooks

★ *The Night Pirates* by Peter Harris

★ *The Pirate Cruncher* by Jonny Duddle

★ *That's Not My Pirate!* by Fiona Watt and Rachel Wells

Observation and assessment

Communication and Language	Expected statements (ELGs)
Listening and attention	Children listen attentively in a range of situations.

Literacy	Expected statements (ELGs)
Reading	Children read and understand simple sentences. They use phonic knowledge to decode regular words and read them aloud accurately. They also read some common irregular words. They demonstrate understanding when talking with others about what they have read.
Writing	Children use their phonic knowledge to write words in ways which match their spoken sounds. They also write some irregular common words. They write simple sentences which can be read by themselves and others. Some words are spelt correctly and others are phonetically plausible.

Key vocabulary

- poster
- Wanted! poster
- features

- character
- belongings
- scarf

- eye-patch
- parrot

What to do

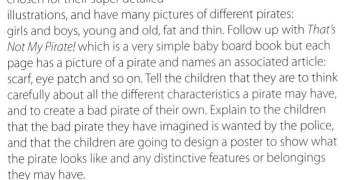

Read the storybooks *The Night Pirates* and *The Pirate Cruncher*. These were chosen for their super detailed illustrations, and have many pictures of different pirates: girls and boys, young and old, fat and thin. Follow up with *That's Not My Pirate!* which is a very simple baby board book but each page has a picture of a pirate and names an associated article: scarf, eye patch and so on. Tell the children that they are to think carefully about all the different characteristics a pirate may have, and to create a bad pirate of their own. Explain to the children that the bad pirate they have imagined is wanted by the police, and that the children are going to design a poster to show what the pirate looks like and any distinctive features or belongings they may have.

Look at some different information posters showing safety advice, items for sale or advertising an event – what do they have in common? What is important to include; conversely what is not necessary?

Discuss the key features of a 'wanted' poster: there is a clear picture of the person missing, with accurate colours used to define eye, hair and skin colour, and possibly labels to show important features: eye patch as he has only one eye/red spotty scarf over hair as her black hair is long down her back. Introduce the key vocabulary, naming body parts, pirate clothing and key possessions that the pirate may have: green parrot on right shoulder, answers to the name Sid! Encourage all children to chat to their response partner in the group, sharing ideas and descriptions of their pirate.

Ask the whole group some 'Thumbs up!' questions to provoke their thoughts and clarify their ideas, e.g. 'Thumbs up if…your pirate is a girl! Your pirate has an eye patch! If it is a red eye patch! If they have an earring! Two earrings!' etc.

Show the children the poster outline and demonstrate drawing a pirate underneath the Wanted! banner. Label some of the key features of the pirate or his belongings.

If this is to be a guided activity…

…then the children can work together with an adult to create their own 'wanted' poster. Use whiteboards to sketch out their pirate before drawing onto paper, talking with the adult about the features and characteristics they have chosen for their pirate. Encourage them to give reasons for their choices.

If this is to be an independent activity…

…then show the children where the collection of collage materials and pictures of faces from magazines are and explain that they can create their pirate sometime this week. Talk to them about how to create the key pirate features – earrings from gold or silver ribbon; beards from wool – and display them on the interactive display when finished.

To support or extend

To support, look through magazines or newspaper supplements for large pictures of different faces. Using a picture of a face, talk about how it could look more like a pirate. Using collage materials add a coloured headscarf from fabric, a black eye patch, glue on a wool beard and draw some scary eyebrows with a black felt tip pen. Encourage the children to tell you what they would like to add to create their pirate face, let them find the fabric or materials (e.g. black curly wool for a beard) and help with the cutting and gluing.

To extend, write a pirate description to be read out on the radio. Record it, and listen to it with other children. Older children could draw a pirate in response to the oral description and the writer of the description could choose the winning pirate most like their imagined character.

Ideas for interactive display

- Put the pirate pictures and 'wanted' posters up as a 'Rogues gallery'! Compare the pictures created and ask the children to comment upon the features used most popularly – are there any pirates without beards? How many female pirates are there? What seems to be the pirates' favourite colour?

- Put out other games and activities which require children to closely observe facial features, e.g. Guess Who; Happy Families; Snap!

Parents and carers as partners

At home, help your child to make a 'wanted' poster for their favourite teddy or doll, or a family pet. Explain that this is what people do when things are lost. This way, whenever your child can't find their teddy they can display the poster for other people at home to use when searching. Look at the teddy, doll or pet together and draw it as accurately as possible. Help your child to think of simple adjectives (e.g. brown, furry, one eye, tail missing) and add these to your poster.

Pirates ahoy!

Pirate moneybags

The children will be using gold coins to count, add and exchange for treasure.

Resources

★ Apron and pirate headscarf (for adult)

★ Smaller pirate hat

★ Shiny 1p coins (real ones clink together nicely, put them in fizzy cola overnight to restore their shine

★ Old socks (moneybags)

★ Items a pirate may need for their sea journey: clothing, maps, telescope, food and drink, parrot food

★ Box large enough to contain these items

★ Treasure for the pirates: broken or old necklaces, belt buckles, pieces of chain, gold or silver coloured plates, bowls or doilies (foil partyware is great), medals or trophies

★ Treasure chest

★ Labels with prices written on, all under 10p

★ Wide strip of paper

★ Calculator

Storybooks

★ *Mrs Pirate (Read Me Storybook)* by Nick Sharratt

★ *The Great Pet Sale* by Mick Inkpen

Observation and assessment

Mathematics	Expected statements (ELGs for end of F2)
Numbers	Children count reliably with numbers from 1 to 20, place them in order and say which number is one more or one less than a given number. Using quantities and objects, they add and subtract two single-digit numbers and count on or back to find the answer. They solve problems, including doubling, halving and sharing.

Key vocabulary

- journey
- voyage
- money
- coins
- gold
- silver
- copper
- moneybags
- purse
- more
- less
- fewer
- how many
- how much

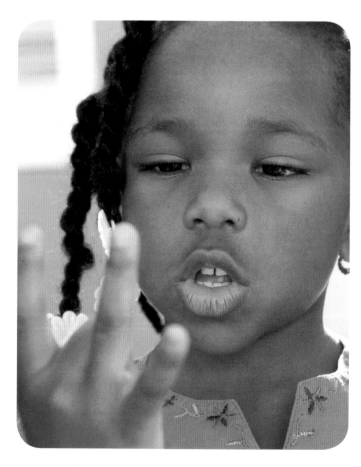

What to do

Come into the room dressed in an apron and pirate headscarf, carrying a large box (to look like a treasure box if possible). Inside the box have a selection of items which a pirate may buy. Also have to hand another (smaller) pirate hat and a sock with some jingly 1p coins. Select a child to wear the pirate hat, and give them the money sock. Explain that they are going on a journey and need to buy some items from the pirate shopkeeper (you!) but that they do not have enough money to buy everything, so they must choose thoughtfully and count their pennies carefully.

Set up the shop on the floor, taking the items from the box and setting them on the floor where the other children can see them. Ensure they all have large price labels so that the remaining children can see the cost.

Discuss what items would be necessary on a voyage: something to wear, something to eat and drink. Allow the pirate child to come up, select something and pay for it carefully. Take it in turns for the other children to wear the hat and count out money from the sock, buying other items. Use the key vocabulary when talking and shopping. When the money has all gone show the children the other treasure chest, looking at the items of treasure. Explain that when a pirate has run out of money he can exchange (swap or trade) some of the treasure he has for money, so that he can go to the shop to buy food. Give the treasure chest to a child. Let them select an item of treasure to swap with you. Take the treasure from the child and say, 'This is worth five pence!' Give them the money to put in the box. Continue with other children, modelling paying with and receiving money, checking the amount by counting each time. Encourage all children to participate in some way so that you can confirm they can count one-to-one with 1p coins.

For extra reinforcement read *The Great Pet Sale* by Mick Inkpen to look at price labels, coins and shopping. If you have enough pennies you can 'pay' for each animal in the story to see how much money the boy spends altogether.

If this is to be a guided activity…

…then the children can work together with an adult to play 'pirate shopping'. With a partner alternate being the shopper and the shopkeeper, paying for the items with the gold coins. Give each child a wide strip of paper so that they can create a 'till receipt' by recording what was bought and how much it cost. At the end help the children to add up the total price of the items purchased to find out who spent the most money.

If this is to be an independent activity…

…then show the children where the box of resources will be, and explain that they can try this activity sometime this week. Provide plenty of pirate gold coins or shiny pennies, a till, a calculator and a small whiteboard. Let the children play at shopping for the pirate items. As an extension set up a pirate café in the room, with a pirate themed food and drink menu (e.g. Salty Sea Soup; Parrot Pie; Crossbones Biscuits) where the children can pay for things and receive change.

To support or extend

To support, simply play 'pirate shops' with one or two children. Use multiples of 1p coins to make up the prices on the pirate items or pirate treasure and take turns to buy and sell, counting out coins. Concentrate on one-to-one counting and the correct sequence of number words.

To extend, investigate how many different combinations of items can be bought with only ten pennies. Provide whiteboards to record, or small gold paper coins for the children to use to work out the answers. For example, two drinks at 5p each, or three 3p biscuits and a 1p map. Help the children to record by using pictures and number symbols to write a number addition sentence.

Ideas for interactive display

- Put up a washing line and peg ten gold coins onto it. Use these to rehearse and consolidate number bonds to ten – use two differently coloured pegs on the line.

- Have a selection of items to peg onto the washing line, each clearly labelled with a price. Keep the numbers small or extend to higher prices to suit your children's ability. Ask the children to 'hang out the pirate washing' in order of price. If you provide different large denomination coins (5p, 10p, 20p) the children can put the items in a basket which total that price as an extension activity.

Parents and carers as partners

At home, collect some shiny 1p coins to use as treasure (soak them in fizzy cola overnight to make them shiny again). Gather together items from around the home that a pirate may need for a journey such as a bandana, a flask and a map. Give these items price labels (under 10p to begin with) and play pirate shopping. Take it in turns to be the pirate, and try to buy different items with your coins. Count aloud when picking up each coin and match the price labels to the number of pennies. Extend to other coins when your child is ready.

Pirates ahoy!

Chilly pirate drinks

The children will be trying to keep an ice cube frozen by testing out different methods of insulation.

Observation and assessment

Understanding the world	Expected statements (ELGs)
The world	Children know about similarities and differences in relation to places, objects, materials and living things. They make observations of animals and plants and explain why some things occur, and talk about changes.

Key vocabulary

- water
- ice
- ice cube
- iceberg
- freezing
- frozen
- thawing
- melting
- melted
- fair test

Resources

★ Ice cubes

★ Newspaper

★ Plates/bowls

★ Styrofoam cups and something to use as a lid

★ Differently shaped large containers

★ Plastic toys to freeze in the ice such as Lego, farm animals etc.

★ Freezer

★ Balloons

Storybooks and non-fiction books

★ *Sid the Science Kid: Why Did My Ice-pop Melt?* by Susan Korman

★ *Why Does Ice Melt?* by Jim Pipe

What to do

Explain to the children that the pirates have a problem when they are sailing the sea – their drinks are never cold enough as their ice cubes always melt. Have an ice cube to put in front of the children whilst you are telling the story so they can watch it slowly disappear. Discuss their experiences of freezing and melting, noting their comments and reactions in order to assess their current level of understanding. Ensure that the children understand that ice is made from frozen water which will melt in a warm environment such as indoors or in the sunshine.

Show the children the different ways they are going to try to keep the ice cube frozen for longer, for example: lay one out individually; lay it on top of others; wrap it in one piece of newspaper; put it in an open Styrofoam cup; put it in a covered Styrofoam cup. Introduce the key vocabulary during the discussion, ensuring all children understand and can use the words freeze, frozen, thaw, melting, melted. Encourage all the children to share their thoughts on which method will keep the ice cube frozen for longer, predicting and trying to give reasons for their predictions.

Show the children the ice cubes (all the same size) and the plates/bowls/cups/newspaper where they will be placed. Explain that each of the differently wrapped cubes need to be placed in the same place (for example on the table in the room) so that the test is fair – if one was in the fridge and one on the radiator it would not be fair.

Demonstrate placing an ice cube into each of the different containers/wrappings and check every few minutes, comparing the size of the remaining ice. Ensure that the children understand that the winner will be the ice cube still frozen after the others are melted.

If this is to be a guided activity...

...then the children can work together with an adult to carry out the activity again. They should now understand about making a test fair and make relatively sensible predictions. Let them choose the methods of keeping the ice cube frozen, where to put them and how to check their melting progress. Throughout the process listen carefully to the children's use of vocabulary to assess their understanding. At the end of the investigation help the children to make a poster to send to the pirates telling them the best place to keep their ice cubes!

If this is to be an independent activity...

...then show the children where the basket of resources is and explain that they can try this activity sometime this week. Have an ice bucket filled with ice cubes for the children to investigate. Provide the resources for them to repeat the activity done as a class or set a new challenge, for example – can they find the warmest and coldest place in the room? Let them carry out fair tests around the room using ice cubes and similar containers. Encourage them to record however they choose – through drawing, notes or the use of ICT (digital camera, flip cameras etc.).

To support or extend

To support, work with a pair of children and let them each choose a different way of keeping the ice cube frozen. Help them to place the ice cube in the appropriate place and keep an eye on it. Whilst waiting for it to melt talk with the children to consolidate their knowledge and understanding of freezing and thawing, noting their use of the correct vocabulary. Encourage them to predict and give reasons for their predictions.

To extend, let the children observe a melting ice balloon, and help them to take measurements from it as it melts, timing the process. Show them how to set a stop clock or sand timer and to look at the balloon every five minutes. Place the balloon on a ruler so that they can measure the length and width of the balloon and note this on a sticky note. Provide a digital camera so that they can also take a photograph at each five minute interval. Put the pictures, photographs and measurements on a timeline to show the changes over time.

Ideas for interactive display

- Put the tuff spot or water tray on the floor near to the display and let the children investigate differently sized pieces of ice. (See if they realise that the larger the piece of ice, the slower it is to melt.) Freeze water in large containers such as a 2 litre drink bottles, balloons, plastic food containers and jelly moulds. The children will love to touch, hold and investigate the differently shaped pieces of ice – particularly the ice balloon!

- If you partially submerge small plastic items in the containers when freezing it (for example by dropping a handful of Lego into the drink bottle, then freezing it lying down) the children will be able to predict which pieces of Lego will be released first when the ice thaws!

Parents and carers as partners

At home, try making some giant icebergs from unusual containers. Fill triangular yoghurt pots, ridged drink bottles, balloons, cake cases, jelly moulds and large butter tubs with water and place them in the freezer. When they are frozen put them in a large bowl or the sink for your child to play with. If you sprinkle salt onto the frozen shapes they will crackle and react by melting in patterns. Submerge small plastic objects (e.g. toy animals, people) in the containers when half frozen and your child can have fun using wooden implements trying to excavate them as if an archaeologist!

Pirates ahoy!

Pirate hats, cutlasses and eye patches

The children will be designing and making a pirate hat, cutlass and eye patch from paper and card.

Observation and assessment

Expressive arts and design	Expected statements (ELGs)
Exploring and using media and materials	They safely use and explore a variety of materials, tools and techniques, experimenting with colour, design, texture, form and function.
Being imaginative	Children use what they have learnt about media and materials in original ways, thinking about uses and purposes. They represent their own ideas, thoughts and feelings through design and technology, art, music, dance, role-play and stories.

Key vocabulary

- hat
- cutlass
- sword
- eye patch
- cut
- shape
- join
- bend
- fold
- thread
- knot
- punch a hole
- staple
- stick
- glue
- decorate

Resources

★ Pictures of cutlasses, pirate hats and eye patches for the reference

★ Sheets of newspaper (broadsheet and/or tabloid) one sheet per child

★ Paper and card of different thicknesses and colours, including black

★ Elastic

★ Tape measure

★ Foil

★ Scissors, hole punch, stapler, sticky tape, glue sticks, treasury tags, split pins and ruler

Storybooks

★ *That's Not My Pirate!* by Fiona Watt and Rachel Wells

★ *Now I Am A Pirate* by Catherine Osborne

What to do

Explain to the children that they are going to make some of the items a pirate may have, and that they are going to measure their own bodies to make sure that the items fit properly. Look at the simple board book *That's Not My Pirate!* or another simple pirate book. Talk about the clothes that pirates wear – explain that they need a hat to keep the sun off their head whilst they are sailing on the sea and a cutlass (or sword) to fend off the enemy. Talk about the fact that pirates may be injured during a fight, and that is why in some stories they have only one eye, leg or arm – hence the eye patch. Introduce the key vocabulary whilst naming the items and showing the pictures of different hats, cutlasses and eye patches. Encourage all children to make a comment during this time, for example when expressing a preference or drawing together similarities or differences from the pictures.

Show the children how to make a simple pirate hat from a sheet of newspaper: see Parents and carers as partners for the simple instructions. Give each child a piece of newspaper and let them copy you at each stage – when it is finished, try it on; does it fit? Or is it too large or too small? Does this mean that when they make their own hat the piece of paper needs to be bigger or smaller? Talk about making the hat again from thicker paper or thin card, and the colours/sizes necessary if it is to fit well.

Repeat demonstrating and making the other items, including an eye patch and/or cutlass. Talk about size and shape, straight and curved, long and short, big and small. Show the children how to measure comparatively (e.g. not big enough, too short, needs to be longer). If they are old enough use the ruler to count and measure using numbers and recognised units of measurement such as centimetres.

If this is to be a guided activity…

…then the children can work together with an adult to create a pirate 'kit' including the three items demonstrated above. Ensure that the children are using the key vocabulary correctly, and are able to measure suitable amounts of paper, card, string and elastic when constructing. Let them have a fairly free rein, and chat with them during the process as they choose materials and methods when designing and making.

If this is to be an independent activity…

…then show the children where the box of resources will be, and explain that they can try this activity sometime this week. Provide many different types, colours and sizes of construction materials so that the children can have the opportunity to explore the properties of different materials. They may wish to attempt making the eye patch from fabric, for example – if this is the case ensure that the scissors provided are sharp enough to cut it.

To support or extend

To support, help the children to measure how long they need their cutlass to be. Have some stencils made up from thick card and let the children lay them out on the floor in size order. Talk together about what they can see, using vocabulary such as straight, curved, long, longer, short, shorter, shortest, tall, tallest. Ask the children to order themselves in a line from tallest to shortest, and then let them choose the cutlass most appropriately sized for them. They can then make one from card by drawing around the template and cutting it out. Wrap the 'blade' in foil to make it look like shiny metal.

To extend, let the children make a different style of hat (for example, a crown) using a hat band which needs to be measured using a ruler and a thin strip of fabric, string or a tape measure. In pairs, help the children to measure around each other's heads with the tape measure, marking on the place where it meets. Show them how to transfer this measurement to a band of card, cutting it off carefully at the necessary point (remember to leave a few centimetres for joining together). Use the individually measured band of card to make a simple crown (cut points into a gold band) or a chef's hat (glue a piece of white crêpe paper inside to create a dome).

Ideas for interactive display

Put some large dolls, teddies or other soft toys on the display table and explain that they need to be dressed up as pirates. Provide all the necessary paper, card and construction materials along with the pictures of different styles of hat and curved cutlass, and let the children design and make appropriately sized pirate kit. When finished the dolls and teddies could be placed along the table in a line from largest to smallest.

Parents and carers as partners

At home, make a simple pirate hat from a single sheet of newspaper:

1. Fold a piece of newspaper in half, bringing the top down over the bottom as if closing a laptop.

2. Fold it left to right (as if closing a book) and then unfold it again – this is only to mark a line in the centre.

3. Fold the top right corner of the rectangle to the bottom of the centre crease you just made. Turn the entire hat over and repeat this on the other side; you now have a triangle shape with the point at the top and the open long length is at the bottom.

4. Fold up a flap or hem at the bottom, using only the top sheet. Turn it over and repeat.

5. Your hat is finished! Secure the folds with tape or glue stick if necessary.

Treasure island

Message in a bottle

The children will be looking at different types of letters and postcards, and writing a note to put in a bottle, to float off into the sea.

Resources

★ Small plastic bottles with screw tops

★ A5 paper in different colours

★ Selection of letters and postcards with pictures of different destinations

★ Large water tray

★ Selection of different bottles, tins and jars with lids, of varying weight , size and shape

★ Collection of holiday brochures showing different locations (e.g. beach, snow, lakes, mountains, cities)

★ Individual whiteboards

★ Digital camera

Storybooks

★ *The Jolly Postman* by Janet and Allan Ahlberg

★ *Katie Morag Delivers the Mail* by Mairi Hedderwick

Key vocabulary

· message	· float	· letter
· letter	· sink	· dear
· bottle	· island	

Observation and assessment

Communication and Language	Expected statements (ELGs)
Listening and attention	Children listen attentively in a range of situations. They give their attention to what others say and respond appropriately, while engaged in another activity.

Literacy	Expected statements (ELGs)
Writing	Children use their phonic knowledge to write words in ways which match their spoken sounds. They also write some irregular common words. They write simple sentences which can be read by themselves and others. Some words are spelt correctly and others are phonetically plausible.

What to do

Explain to the children that when people are lost on an island at sea there are no telephones or computers to contact the rest of the world to tell people where you are. Ask the children how they could tell someone how they are when they are far away – have any of them ever written a postcard to send from holiday? Talk about putting a stamp on and posting it. Discuss what would happen if there were no postal service – how could they get their message delivered? Show them a bottle, and explain that people have been known to write a letter and put it inside a bottle, put the lid on and put it in the sea. What do they think would happen to the bottle and to the message? Why is it important to put the lid on – what would happen if the lid was left off? Introduce the key vocabulary.

Show the children the A5 sized pieces of paper. Demonstrate tearing around the edges of the paper to make it look old and worn. Ask the children what they would need to put in their message so that they would be found and rescued: a drawing of their island for the rescuers; how long they had been there; a symbol to say what the weather would be like! Encourage the children to give suggestions of their own. On the flipchart demonstrate writing a letter, putting the name of the person you are sending it to at the top. At each stage of letter writing explain to the children what you are doing and why. Write one or two simple sentences, e.g. 'I am lost on an island. It has two trees.' Draw a picture or two to show where you are (draw two trees) or what the weather is like (a sun or raincloud).

If this is to be a guided activity…

…then the children can work together with an adult to write their letters, put them into bottles and practise floating them in the water tray. Help the children to tear the edges of their paper first before writing so that they do not tear their writing or pictures. Have the key features and simple sentences of a letter written onto different card strips (e.g. Dear Mummy/Love from /It is sunny/I am lost/The island has two trees etc.) Help the children to choose the correct phrases to write onto their letters, illustrating appropriately. Children can sort and copy the appropriate phrases or attempt to write independently, using phonetically plausible attempts at their spellings.

If this is to be an independent activity…

…then show the children where the collection of bottles, jars and tins are and let them choose to investigate these at some time over the week. Provide different sizes and colours of paper for writing the letters along with crayons and felt tips for drawing pictures and scenes. Talk to the children about how important it is that the bottle or container must float so that the message is carried by the sea. Put the water tray out so that when the children have created a letter they can investigate which container will float or sink, and which has the capacity to contain their letter. Record on individual whiteboards or with the digital camera.

To support or extend

To support, give the children a blank postcard and explain that they are going to create a picture of a location by selecting photographs from a holiday brochure and cutting them out to glue onto a blank postcard. Talk with the children about what type of place they are lost in – is it hot or cold, wet or dry, beach or mountain. What can they see from where they are? Explain that the pictures they select from the brochure must give other people clues to their destination. Encourage the children to write 'Dear' and the name of the recipient as well as 'From' and their own name.

To extend, ask the children to create a type of 'time capsule' from items to give clues to their location. Explain that there is nothing to write with where they are so they need to gather together some objects to give clues to their location. For example, if they were on the beach what could they put inside the bottle to give clues (sand, shells, seaweed etc). Go outside and look for objects in the local environment that are typical of the location.

Ideas for interactive display

- Have a postcard display wall – encourage children to bring in any postcards or letters they have received from others to share with the group. If this topic is delivered around a holiday period give all the children an adhesive label with the setting address on so that they can send a postcard to the setting from somewhere else.

- Provide a stack of blank postcards along with crayons, stickers, glue sticks and pages from holiday travel brochures. Let the children create their own postcards and add hand drawn sticker stamps or if you have a stamper they can even frank their own postmarks!

Parents and carers as partners

At home, try to find a postcard showing an area you are familiar with or have visited on holiday. Help your child to draw and write on it and actually send it to someone you know. Let your child experience putting on a stamp and putting it in the post-box, and then when it is received by the other person let the child see it again. Alternatively use a blank postcard for your child to draw a picture on. Encourage other people to send postcards to your children so they can make a collection with different images.

Treasure island

Treasure map maths

The children will be using coordinates to find treasure hidden under a cloth.

Observation and assessment

Mathematics	Expected statements (ELGs)
Numbers	Children count reliably with numbers from 1 to 20, place them in order and say which number is one more or one less than a given number. They solve problems, including doubling, halving and sharing.
Shape, space and measures	Children use everyday language to talk about size, weight, capacity, position, distance, time and money to compare quantities and objects and to solve problems.

Key vocabulary

- grid
- reference
- coins
- coordinate
- treasure
- jewellery

Resources

★ Treasure: gold and silver coins, jewellery, picture frames, a belt with buckle, a pirates' hook

★ Large cloth

★ Four canes/metre rulers/heavy pieces of rope to lay over the cloth to create the grid

★ Card labels for the coordinates: ABC 123

★ Example of a simple map with a basic grid of coordinates (from a shopping centre or a playground park)

★ Paper with large squares (at least 2 cm by 2 cm)

★ Laminated simple grids approximately A4 size

★ Dry wipe pens

★ Chalk

★ Outside space

Storybooks

★ *The Pirate Treasure Map: A Fairytale Adventure* by Colin and Jacqui Hawkins

★ *The Treasure of Captain Claw* by Jonathan Emmett

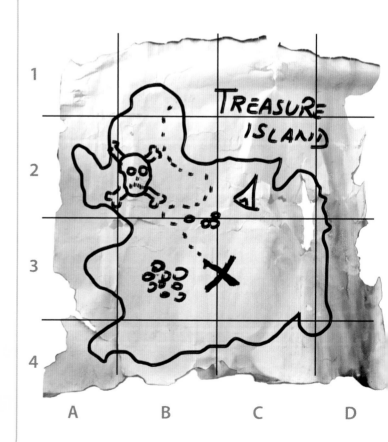

What to do

Show the children the maps. Ask they them how they could find a place on the map – how would they know where it was? And if they were going to tell their friend how would they describe its location? Explain that some maps have lines on them to make little squares, and that each square has a reference as a name. Lay out the canes on the floor making a simple grid (like a noughts and crosses grid). Put three or four items of 'treasure' (a chocolate foil wrapped coin, a necklace, a silver doily, a foil 'silver' dish) onto the grid, one in each square. Decide which is the top of the grid and sit the children at the bottom of it. Lay out the letter cards first along the bottom of the grid, saying the letters A, B, C as you put them down. Tell the children that each of the columns is called A, B or C. Check their understanding by asking, 'What is in column A?''Which column is the necklace in?' When you are confident that the children are comfortable with this concept put the numbers up the side; 1, 2, and 3. Explain that the rows are numbered 1, 2 and 3 and ask questions of the children as before. Show them how to point at the object and move their fingers away to the left and below to identify the coordinate, e.g. B1.

Let the children demonstrate their knowledge by asking each other questions about the location of different items, using the key vocabulary correctly. Encourage all children to either ask or answer a question to prove their understanding. Explain that by giving a place on a map a coordinate (name) it is possible to find hidden treasure! Remove all the treasure from the grid and throw a cloth over the cane grid. Now tell the children that you are going to 'bury' some treasure in one of the squares, but they won't know which one, they will have to have lots of guesses to find out. Put a piece of (flat) treasure secretly under the cloth. Choose a child to give you a coordinate to check. Look under the cloth and say yes or no. Keep a list of coordinates suggested on the flipchart, or draw a simple grid and draw X in the squares identified.

If this is to be a guided activity...

...then the children can work together with an adult playing treasure hunt maps. Use the cloth in the same way to hide the treasure but let the children run the activity whilst you suggest coordinates. Check that they can record appropriately on the grid. This activity can be played outside on a larger scale. Chalk a grid onto the ground, adding labels along each axis. Blindfold a child, then ask several other children to run onto the grid and stand in a square. Make sure they know what the coordinate of their square is. Ask the blindfolded child to shout out a coordinate – if they say one that a child is standing in then that child takes a turn as the blindfolded one.

If this is to be an independent activity...

...then show the children where the box of treasure, the canes and the cloth will be and explain that they can try this activity sometime this week. Have a flipchart with several grids drawn on it for the children to record when they have played the game. By asking them to draw what the treasure actually was in the correct square you have evidence that they have played the game. Miniature versions of this for pairs to play can be made to keep in a small wallet using a tea towel, two small laminated grids with coordinate labels (one to hide under the cloth, another to write on with a dry wipe pen) and some chocolate coins. The winner can eat the treasure!

To support or extend

To support, play this game with one or two children on a bigger scale so that the children can actually walk into the squares. Chalk out the grid on the ground and walk around it, saying the names of the squares as you hop from one to the next. Ask the children to go and stand in certain squares (e.g. 'Ben, please stand in A1') or have the coordinates written on postcards for the children to choose and then go and stand in. Work in pairs so that one child can check the other is in the correct position.

To extend, play this as a paper and pen game, similar to battleships. Let each child make their own grid on squared paper or a whiteboard (if you make a grid onto A4 paper and photocopy it the grids can be laminated and used with a dry wipe pen many times). Have a master copy and give each square point values of 1, 2 and 3. Let the children choose a coordinate – write the value attributed to that square on the flipchart. The children can add up the values they achieve, taking it in turns until all squares are chosen. The winner is the one with the highest score.

Ideas for interactive display

- Put the resources for the main activity on the display table for the children to play at any time. Provide the small wallets with laminated grids and chocolate coins for the children to select to play as a pair as an independent activity.

- Outside, provide chalk for the children to investigate making their own grids of different sizes and scales by drawing on the ground.

- Display maps and plans of different scales, colours and made for different purposes for the children to look at and talk about. If possible try to display maps of places familiar to the children.

Parents and carers as partners

At home, play a game using positional language (e.g. next to, behind, left, right, in front of, between etc.) where your child tries to find an object you have hidden. Secretly put a small object somewhere visible in a room and let your child be directed to it by following instructions (a 2p coin is perfect for this). For example, send your child out of the room and put the 2p coin in plain view on the edge of a shelf/top of the spine of a book/laid on a similar coloured cushion. Bring your child back into the room, stand them in the doorway and give instructions: it is next to the television/in front of the sofa/between the books. The coin can be surprisingly difficult to spot. Encourage your child to ask questions when trying to locate it.

Treasure island

Raft racing!

The children will be looking at different types of boat, and making a raft from straws in order to win a raft race.

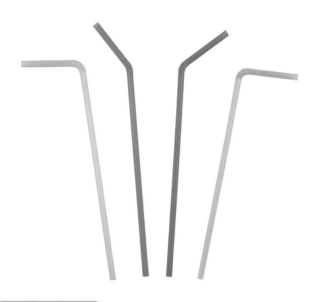

Observation and assessment

Understanding the world	Expected statements (ELGs)
The world	Children know about similarities and differences in relation to places, objects, materials and living things. They make observations of animals and plants and explain why some things occur, and talk about changes.

Key vocabulary

- boat
- raft
- ship
- yacht
- catamaran
- dinghy
- rowing boat
- canoe
- kayak
- ferry

Resources

★ Pictures of different styles of boat (internet, books or magazines)

★ Pictures of different rafts, including some simple rafts from other cultures

★ Selection of straws of different sizes and widths

★ Making tape/sticky tape

★ Scissors

★ Large scale construction for outdoors (poles, sticks, canes, blocks, planks, ropes)

★ Large water tray

Storybooks

★ *Jack's Big Race* by Michael Foreman

★ *Brer Anansi and the Boat Race: A Folk Tale from the Caribbean* by David P. Makhanlall

What to do

Show the children the pictures of different types of boat. Ask them to give you as many different names for types of boat as possible and draw up a list on the flipchart. Ensure they are able to use and understand the key vocabulary. Explain that a very simple boat can be made by joining together some poles or tree trunks with rope to make a floating raft. Show them the pictures of simple rafts from other cultures, talking about the similarities and differences between them. Remind children that wood is often used because it is a natural, available material and that it floats. Show the children the selection of straws and talk about how they could make a raft. What would they need to ensure? (That it was wide enough to float, that the straws were securely joined together, that the straws were the same length.)

Discuss how to achieve this – demonstrate measuring the straws against each other before cutting them. Talk about the different straws – encourage the children to consider what would happen if they used a mixture of straws with a different diameter. Encourage all children to think and to contribute to the discussion, either independently or through a response partner. Demonstrate making a raft and joining with tape. Finally explain to the children that they are going to take part in a raft race on the water tray with their completed rafts.

If this is to be a guided activity...

...then the children can work together with an adult to build their rafts with support. Show them how to cut the straws, position the tape and join together. Provide the opportunity to test the rafts on the water tray to make sure that they do not sink before entering the race. To race the boats, try them a few at a time by placing them at one end of the water tray and then creating a wave (by tipping up the tray slightly). Which one reaches the other side first?

If this is to be an independent activity...

...then show the children where the basket of resources is and explain that they can try this activity sometime this week. As well as making a raft that will simply float along, provide differently sized small world objects, animals and people for the children to carry as passengers and cargo. Explore what size and shape raft will carry which cargo. Record with pictures on the whiteboard.

To support or extend

To support, take the children into a small space and help them to use the large equipment to build a raft big enough to 'carry' them. Explain that they can't actually test it on the water but that they can build one together and then make a model of it. Use the poles, planks, sticks and canes and join with rope, or use a collection of large tubes such as those from paper rolls or even carpet rolls. Count how many were used in the big model before helping the children to replicate the model with the same number of straws.

To extend, provide the children with a challenge. Give them a piece of cargo that is difficult to transport, either because it is large, strangely shaped or unwieldy. Challenge pairs of children to use the fewest number of straws possible to build a boat suitable for carrying the cargo. Test it together as a small group.

Ideas for interactive display

- Put pictures of many different types of boat on the display table. Provide a basket of small world people for counting/toy bears/dinosaurs or similar. Ask the children to order the pictures along the floor by how many people each craft can carry – e.g. kayak (one), canoe (two), rowing boat (around three or four) up to boat, ferry and ship. It does not matter if they are not exactly accurate, but they should demonstrate a broad understanding.

- Provide a selection of straws and tape next to the water tray so that the children can investigate design and load during free play.

Parents and carers as partners

At home, look for pictures of different types of boats and make a large sea picture. Obtain a large free sample of blue or green wallpaper from a DIY shop to use as the sea background. Cut out pictures of any boats you can find from magazines, holiday brochures and toy catalogues. Glue these onto the large piece of wallpaper any way you like. Attach the blue wallpaper to the wall and develop the frieze over a week or two.

Treasure island

Pirate dancing

The children will be making a pirate dance, by climbing the rigging, scrubbing the decks and looking for land ahoy!

Resources

* ★ Sailing boat (or a picture of one)

* ★ Multiple small pictures of boat parts (rigging, deck, wheel and crow's nest)

* ★ Flipchart

* ★ Blu tack

* ★ Selection of percussion instruments

* ★ Flip camera (or similar)

* ★ Dictophone or sound recorder

Songs

* ★ 'What shall we do with a drunken sailor?' (Traditional song)

* ★ 'A Sailor Went To Sea, Sea, Sea' (action rhyme)

Observation and assessment

Expressive arts and design	Expected statements (ELGs)
Exploring and using media and materials	They safely use and explore a variety of materials, tools and techniques, experimenting with colour, design, texture, form and function.
Being imaginative	Children use what they have learnt about media and materials in original ways, thinking about uses and purposes. They represent their own ideas, thoughts and feelings through design and technology, art, music, dance, role-play and stories.

Key vocabulary

* · sails
* · decks
* · rigging

* · crow's nest
* · ship's wheel
* · pattern

* · sequence

What to do

Explain to the children that pirates need to carry out lots of tasks when they are sailing the seas to keep their boat safe and seaworthy. Look at the model (or picture) of the sailing boat and make sure that the children know what the different parts of the boat are called and what they are used for, introducing the key vocabulary. Discuss how these actions could be modelled by the children even if they do not have a boat. Make a list of around four parts of the boat: rigging, decks, crow's nest, and ship's wheel. Talk about what they are used for and how the children can mime the action: climb the rigging/scrub the decks/look through a telescope in the crow's nest and steer the ship by turning the wheel. Encourage all the children to join in the actions. Identify one or two children that are very good at each action and let them show the other children their action. Comment upon why it is good: do they bend down low/stretch up high/use both hands?

Show some simple pictures of the boat parts to prompt the children to perform the action. Can they watch the pictures and do it without any prompting? Put some of the pictures on the flipchart in a pattern: rigging/decks/rigging/decks/wheel. Tell the children that they are going to make a dance by joining the actions in a sequence. Count or clap for four or eight beats so that the children know how long they are going to perform the action before they change to the next action. If you want to put these actions to music choose a simple piece of music in 4/4 time (with four beats to a bar) with a clear beat, which you can count aloud over so that the children know when to change action.

If this is to be a guided activity…

…then the children can work together with an adult to create their own dance sequence. Use the small pictures of the parts of the boat to prompt the children which action is next. Let them rearrange the pictures in different sequences and explore the different dances resulting from this. Ask them to give reasons for their choices and amend their selection where necessary.

If this is to be an independent activity…

…then show the children where the selection of pictures are and let them use these to create their own sequences of movement to put into a dance. Encourage the children to take turns at being the dance choreographer, sequencing the pictures on the flipchart, pointing and clapping out the beat for the other children to follow. Have a sash, a waistcoat or a hat for the choreographer to wear. Let the children record using a flip camera or similar.

To support or extend

To support, sing the song 'This is the way we scrub the decks/climb the rigging/turn the wheel/look for land… On a pirate ship in the morning' to the tune of 'Here we go round the Mulberry Bush'. Show the children the action for each verse, and have a picture clue to point to when it is time to sing it. Let them make up extra verses of their own with matching verses: walk the plank/swim to shore/count the treasure.

To extend, provide some percussion instruments for the children so they can add sound effects to their actions. Talk with them about what would be the most suitable instrument to represent, for example, the action of scrubbing the decks – something to make a swishing sound. Use these sounds as they did the actions: put them in a sequence, make a pattern with the sounds or repeat them as an echo. Record the music either on a camera or with a sound recorder.

Ideas for interactive display

- Put the selection of pictures out on the display table for the children to sequence and play with. Let the children look at the dance sequences recorded on the flip cameras and try to replicate these.

- Provide a sticky note pad for the children to add their own actions by drawing, e.g. walk the plank/ swim to shore/count the treasure. Let them record these also as a short film so that they can show the other children for a critique.

Parents and carers as partners

At home, make some actions for simple everyday routines such as cleaning teeth, brushing hair or getting dressed. Sing to the tune of 'Here we go round the Mulberry Bush', doing the actions in turn. Let your child think of other actions they perform, e.g. 'This is the way we walk up the stairs/eat our toast/wave goodbye' and sing at every opportunity! Lots of simple songs can be adapted by adding your own personal phrases, however silly – try 'If you're happy and you know it eat your peas!'

Sand and sea

Beach safety poster

The children will be talking about safety on the beach, and making a poster showing how to keep safe.

Resources

* ★ Examples of safety posters and leaflets
* ★ Pieces of A3 or larger coloured paper
* ★ A4 paper (folded into thirds)
* ★ Glue sticks
* ★ Scissors
* ★ Sunhats/sun cream/sun umbrella/swimsuit, wetsuit or sun-suit cover-up
* ★ Bottles of water
* ★ Armband/swimming floats
* ★ Holiday brochures (for family holidays in the sun) and summer clothing catalogues
* ★ Digital camera

Storybooks

* ★ *Hari at the Beach! (Hari Child Safety Awareness)* by Tristan McGee
* ★ *Safety Dave and Daisy Go To The Beach* by David McNutt
* ★ *Near Water (Safety First)* by Ruth Thomson
* ★ *Sea Rescue Services (Emergency 999)* by Kathryn Walker

Observation and assessment

Communication and Language	Expected statements (ELGs)
Speaking	Children express themselves effectively, showing awareness of listeners' needs. They use past, present and future forms accurately when talking about events that have happened or are to happen in the future. They develop their own narratives and explanations by connecting ideas or events.
Understanding	They answer 'how' and 'why' questions about their experiences and in response to stories or events.

Literacy	Expected statements (ELGs)
Writing	Children use their phonic knowledge to write words in ways which match their spoken sounds. They also write some irregular common words. They write simple sentences which can be read by themselves and others. Some words are spelt correctly and others are phonetically plausible.

Key vocabulary

• safe	• sun cream	• coastguard
• sun	• sunburn	• poster
• sea	• rescue	
• sunhat	• lifeguard	

What to do

Explain to the children that they are going to make a poster to tell other children how to stay safe at the beach. There are some accidents which can happen on a beach which are mostly preventable, and the children are going to teach other (younger) children about them. If it possible, arrange for an adult who works with younger children in the setting to pop in to formally request that the children 'help' her to teach the younger children about beach safety.

Discuss what going to the beach is like. Encourage the children who have been to a beach, either in England or abroad to share their experiences with the other children (remain sensitive to any children who may not have any direct experience of visits to the seaside). Make a list of keywords on the flipchart related to what it is like, e.g. hot, sunny, busy, lots of people, the sea has waves etc. Show the children the selection of items you have brought in that are linked to the beach and the sun: sunhat, armbands, sun cream, water bottle, sun umbrella etc. Choose one item and explain how it could be useful on the beach to keep a child safe; 'This sun hat will keep the sun off my head.' Introduce the key vocabulary, encouraging all children to choose an item and say a sentence about its usefulness on the beach. Explain that as they are going to teach the younger children about beach safety they will need to draw bright, clear pictures showing what would be useful and why. Remind them that the younger children probably cannot read. Demonstrate on the flipchart a drawing of a child wearing a sun hat and armbands. Draw a large tick at the side to show this is desirable. Alternatively draw a child with red sunburn and no hat, and add a large red cross through the picture to indicate that this is wrong. Talk with the children about what they are going to include on their poster and how they are going to show it. Make a list of keywords that will be useful to the children on the flipchart so they can copy the words they require. Show the children the holiday brochures and explain that they can cut out any pictures they think would be useful on their poster.

If this is to be a guided activity…

…then the children can work together with an adult to create a poster which would be useful to share with younger children, teaching beach safety. Work in two teams on separate large pieces of paper, one headed with a large green tick for recommended behaviour and the other headed with a large red cross for unsafe behaviour. Invite the children to select an item from the collection and explain what they know about it. Help them to record on the sheet.

If this is to be an independent activity…

…then show the children where the collection of holiday brochures/catalogues, scissors and glue sticks are and explain that they are to work as a large group over the week to make a collection of pictures of children playing safely on the beach. Provide a large piece of paper and encourage the children to look through the brochures/catalogues to find and cut out pictures/photographs illustrating beach safety. Display these on the interactive display for other children to add to and look at.

To support or extend

To support, use a digital camera to take photographs of the children modelling safe beach behaviour. For example, they could be standing under the beach umbrella, pretending to put on sun cream, wearing a sun hat or inflatable armbands. Print out the pictures or show them on an interactive whiteboard. Ask each child in turn to talk about themselves in the photographs, saying what is important about the items they are wearing or protected by.

To extend, help the children to make a folded leaflet from A4 paper to teach beach safety. Fold the paper length ways to make three sections, show the children the front cover; open it out and show the three sections inside. Help them to write three headings: sun safety/water safety/crowd safety (not getting lost). Write, draw or make a collage under each heading to give information to other people.

Ideas for interactive display

- Display the posters created by the children alongside other types of safety poster. Often charities have information or safety posters (Royal Society for the Prevention of Cruelty to Animals, Royal Society for the Prevention of Aaccidents) available to download or send off for.

- Put out differently sized and folded pieces of paper for the children to use to make their own posters and leaflets about any topic they wish. Provide some way of attaching them to the wall so that the children can display them for the other children to look at.

Parents and carers as partners

At home, talk about keeping safe when out and about. Tell your child what to do if they should ever become separated from you in a shop (never leave the shop; find a person with a shop uniform on and tell her you are lost); or lost in an open public space (on the park or beach – find another family and tell them you are lost). Teach your child your full name, so you can be asked for over a shop loudspeaker (there are a lot of 'mummy's out there!) and teach them their own name, address and telephone number. These 'stranger danger' chats do not have to be frightening, simply role-play 'shops' or 'telephoning home' so your child can practise what to do.

Safety first!

To keep children safe use role-play games to teach them their own name, address and telephone number.

Sand and sea

Making fruit salad

The children will be cutting fruit into halves, quarters and thirds to share out and make fruit salad.

Resources

* Selection of soft fruit (banana, pear, melon, apple, pineapple, oranges, mango)

* Safety knives

* Paper plates/bowls/cups

* Larger bowl for fruit salad

* Pictures of pirates to represent picnic guests

Safety first!
Ensure that none of the children have allergies to any of the foods being prepared or eaten.

* Pirate hats

* Picnic rug

* Coloured play dough

* Labels showing: half ½ ; quarter ¼ : third ⅓

* Simple coloured card outlines of fruit (circles/banana/pear shapes) cut into halves, quarters and thirds

Storybooks

* *Oliver's Fruit Salad* by Vivian French

Observation and assessment

Mathematics	Expected statements (ELGs)
Numbers	Children count reliably with numbers from 1 to 20, place them in order and say which number is one more or one less than a given number. They solve problems, including doubling, halving and sharing.
Space, shape and measures	Children use everyday language to talk about size, weight, capacity, position, distance time and money to compare quantities and objects and to solve problems.

Key vocabulary

* whole
* half
* quarter
* third
* share
* cut
* slice
* count
* divide

What to do

Explain that the pirates are having a party and preparing their own food, but that they need the children's help to make sure that there is enough fruit to go around. Have two oranges, peeled, for the children to look at. Explain to the children that the pirates need to share out the fruit so that it is fair. Choose two children to pretend to be pirates and explain that you are going to share out an orange between them. Give one small segment of orange to one child and the remaining nine tenths of the orange to the other child. Listen to the laughter and howls of outrage! Is that fair? Why not? What would make it fair? Half each? Retrieve the orange from the children and redistribute, half each. Write half and ½ on the flipchart, explaining that this is how it is recorded. Repeat this demonstration with a different fruit showing quarters and thirds. Explain each time how many pirates it would feed equally (four and three respectively). Discuss what a fruit salad is and show the children the different fruits available for them to put into their fruit salads. Talk about each one, ensuring that the children know what they are called, how to cut/peel/prepare them and what they look like inside. Introduce the key vocabulary. Show the children a small number of pirate pictures, e.g. two or three. Spread out the rug and pictures. Choose a child to give each pirate picture a paper plate. Explore cutting and sharing the fruit different ways, talking about how to share fairly and how to cut the fruit into equal sizes. Demonstrate this for the children to use later, independently.

If this is to be a guided activity…

…then the children can work together with an adult to create a fruit salad for the pirates. Have a selection of pirate pictures and paper plates to share out each fruit. Tip it into a large shared bowl at the end of the maths activity. If you give each child a pirate hat they could assume the identity of one of the pirates in the pictures and eat their share!

If this is to be an independent activity…

…then show the children the differently coloured play dough, knives, plates, pirate pictures and fruit pictures and explain that they are to use these independently to make fruit salad from play dough to feed different numbers of pirates. By laminating simple outlines of a whole fruit alongside sections or slices of fruit it is possible for the children to use these as play dough mats; cutting and rolling the play dough into different fractions and writing numerals with a whiteboard pen.

To support or extend

To support, give the children paper shapes to represent the fruit, e.g. a green circle for an apple, a yellow curved shape for a banana, two paper plates, scissors and a glue stick. Explain to each child that they are going to cut their fruit in half to share it with another pirate and glue the pieces fairly onto their two plates. Use the key vocabulary frequently, ensuring that the children understand what a half is.

To extend, help the children to use fractions to work out how many pieces of fruit will be needed for different numbers of pirate guests. For example, take the first example as all pieces of fruit are cut into two, and will need to feed two pirates. How many pieces of fruit will they each receive? If all pieces of fruit are cut into four and still need to feed two pirates how many pieces of fruit will they then receive? Can the children see a pattern? This activity will work best with a very small group of children and possibly use play dough to represent the fruit pieces, as it is difficult to imagine without props.

Ideas for interactive display

- Put out objects and bowls to represent bowls for children to share out. For example, use a handful of beads to represent grapes and children's photographs to represent them. Let the children choose who they are going to share with, put out enough bowls for each photograph and divide the beads or counters representing the food between the children.

- Provide small whiteboards or sticky shapes and paper for the children to draw how they worked it out. These can be photocopied to represent good examples of children's emergent mathematics.

- At snack time use the actual food as real life examples of problem solving maths. Slices of toast or bread and butter cut into different shapes (triangles, rectangles, squares) are perfect for introducing simple fractions.

Parents and carers as partners

At home, let your child help with preparing and serving food to you and other people in your family. Use questions to help them to understand, e.g. 'How many people are there? How many plates will we need? Do we need any more? Do we have enough for one each?' If they are a little older talk about sharing biscuits or fruit by division, e.g. 'We have six grapes but there are only two of us, how many can we have each?' Help your child to share practically, counting along 'One for you, one for me!'

Sand and sea

Ocean in a bottle

The children will be looking at the properties of oil and water, and using them to make an ocean in a bottle.

Resources

* ★ Small clear plastic bottles with screw lids (one per child)
* ★ Glue
* ★ Blue food colouring
* ★ Oil
* ★ Water
* ★ Small shells which fit through the neck of the bottle
* ★ Glitter
* ★ Sand

Storybooks

* ★ *Ocean* by Maurice Pledger
* ★ *Ocean (Eye Wonder)* by Samantha Gray

Observation and assessment

Understanding the world	Expected statements (ELGs)
The world	Children know about similarities and differences in relation to places, objects, materials and living things. They make observations of animals and plants and explain why some things occur, and talk about changes.

Key vocabulary

• sea	• water	• separate
• ocean	• oil	• shells
• waves	• mix	• sand

What to do

Explain to the children that they are going to make an ocean of their own which they can keep in a bottle to play with. Show them the resources needed (oil, water, food colouring and sand). Discuss with them what they think each object is for – what do each of the things represent? Show them a finished bottle with all the ingredients inside, screwed tightly up and move it slowly so that they can see the oils and water sloshing up and down the bottle when it is held horizontally. Explain that this is how waves move on the ocean. Introduce the key vocabulary and move the bottle vigorously to mix the oil, water and sand together. Sit quietly and encourage the children to watch as the mixture separates into its constituent parts, sinking to the bottom or rising to the top. Discuss why this may happen. Draw parallels with experiences the children may have had if they have paddled in the sea – the sand and shells sink to the bottom as they are heavier than the water. Explain that the oil doesn't mix because it likes to join all together and that is why it is in one piece on top of the water.

If this is to be a guided activity…

…then the children can work together with an adult to make the ocean in a bottle. Put out the resources and let them choose a few shells, pebbles, sand and glitter to put in their dry bottle through the neck. Add the coloured water to about half-way and finally add the oil to sit in a thin layer on the top. Fix the lid firmly onto the bottle and let each child experiment with mixing and moving their ocean. Encourage them to be patient whilst waiting for the contents to settle again. Display the oceans on a windowsill where the sunlight can shine through the coloured water.

If this is to be an independent activity…

…then explain to the children that they can make an underwater world on a larger scale in the water tray. Put out a selection of objects for the children to choose from, including natural materials found locally (e.g. pebbles, stones, twigs, shells and pinecones) and those of a more exotic nature (large, brightly coloured shells, coral and natural sponges). Encourage the children to create a small world for the plastic fish, creatures and people to play and swim in. If it possible to buy a cheap disposable underwater camera, help the children to take some photographs under the water of their scenes.

To support, play parachute games where you create waves of different sizes and frequency. Show the children how to move the parachute slowly and gently, then quickly and fiercely. Put a lightweight ball on top of the parachute and let the children lift and tilt their section of the parachute to make the ball ('boat') roll around on top of the 'sea'. Tell a weather story, where the day begins quietly and the sea is calm, but then the wind picks up, and the waves become bigger and fiercer until the wind drops and the sea is calm again.

To extend, use a large flat container such as a tray, paddling pool or Tuff spot outside for the children to practise making waves in. Fill it with water and show the children how to tilt one end slightly in order to make a wave travel down the tray. What happens when it reaches the end? Does it roll back? How else can they make waves? Can they create waves by dropping something into the water? How is this wave pattern different?

Ideas for interactive display

- Display pictures and photographs of underwater scenes, such as coral reefs, deep oceans and garden ponds.

- Put out shallow trays of differently coloured water and let the children choose different objects to half submerge in the water – can they make a small world adventure course for the play people, or an exciting environment for some penguins at the zoo?

Parents and carers as partners

At home, make your own underwater world in a bottle or jar with a lid. Let your child decide what sort of objects they would like in their watery world – stones from the garden, grass, twigs, and petals, or toys, Lego and other manufactured items. Add food colouring to change the colour of the water to transform the atmosphere!

Sand and sea

Beach music!

The children will be using natural materials found on a beach and percussion instruments to make some beach music.

Observation and assessment

Expressive arts and design	Expected statements (ELGs)
Exploring and using media and material	Children sing songs, make music and dance, and experiment with ways of changing them.
Being imaginative	They represent their own ideas, thoughts and feelings through design and technology, art, music, dance, role-play and stories.

Key vocabulary

- shake
- tap
- rattle
- hit
- drum
- move
- clap
- stamp

Resources

★ Selection of objects from the beach (shells, sand and water in different plastic containers to shake; pieces of driftwood and pinecones)

★ Selection of musical percussion instruments including different types of shakers, bells, claves, castanets, coconut shells, rainsticks and wood blocks

★ Small pictures of each percussion instrument, laminated on card

Storybooks

★ *Pat a Cake, Make and Shake: Make and Play Your Own Musical Instruments (Songbooks)* by Sue Nicholls

★ *Musical Instruments (World of Design)* by Ruth Thomson.

What to do

Ask the children to listen silently to the noises around them in their setting, what can they hear? Make a list together on a flipchart. Talk to the children about the sounds they might hear if they were playing on a beach: discuss the sound the sea makes, what the weather might be like and what creatures may be around. Would there be any sounds they would hear on a beach that they would not hear in their local environment, or vice versa? Show the children a selection of natural materials that could have been collected on a beach: shells of different sizes, sand in a plastic container, water in a plastic bottle, pieces of driftwood and pine cones. Explain to the children that they are going to experiment with these objects to make some beach music. Show them how to shake, tap and rattle the objects either independently or against one another to make sounds. Introduce the key vocabulary and talk with the children about the sounds they are making – what do they remind the children of? Encourage all the children to participate. The children may use their bodies and voices to make sounds from the beach too.

Show the children the selection of percussion instruments. Give them time to explore the different sounds each one makes when played. Using the correct name for each instrument try to match the sounds made by the natural materials to the actual percussion instruments. Demonstrate how to play each instrument correctly.

If this is to be a guided activity…

…then the children can work together with an adult to play the instruments in turn and tell a beach story through music. Identify several key sounds that may be heard on a beach, e.g. the waves, children playing, people walking, fish swimming. Encourage the children to decide which instrument or vocal sound will describe each action. As the adult tells a story (or describes a beach scene) the children with the relevant instruments play in the appropriate place. Continue to revise or alter sounds which the children think could be improved. Perform to the other children in the setting. Can they guess what the sounds represent?

If this is to be an independent activity…

…then show the children where the box of resources will be, and explain that they can try this activity sometime this week. Provide multiple copies of photographs of each instrument and show the children how to put these out in a line to tell the musicians which order to play them in. Show one child how to be the conductor and let them point with a drumstick to each photograph when they require that instrument to play. Extend this to timing by saying that as long as the conductor is pointing to a particular photograph then the instrument continues to play.

To support or extend

To support, group the instruments and natural materials by the sound they make. For example, gather together the objects that make a rattling sound like shells in a wave, or a rushing sound like the sea. Allow each child to select their favourite sound and try to group it with something else that makes a similar sound. Ask the children if they can make similar sounds with their bodies or mouths.

To extend, draw a musical score for another group to follow. Begin by drawing and labelling the objects that will be used in the piece of music and making photocopies of these. The children can then arrange these in order of appearance in the piece of music, or they can use a large piece of lining paper to act as a linear 'score' by drawing shapes and symbols to describe how they want the instruments to play. For example, wavy lines for shaking, big circles for hitting etc. Let the children make their own decisions and actions in the music.

Ideas for interactive display

Put a selection of instruments out on the display table for the children to explore. This works even better outside where they can be as noisy as they like!

Provide sorting hoops for the children to group the instruments however they like. Encourage them to discuss the reasons for their choices – they may be simple (e.g. 'These are blue/These are shiny') or they may be more complex (e.g. 'These are plucked/struck/made from metal/have strings'). To extend the children's thinking provide card labels for the hoops so the children have to read and decide where to place them.

Parents and carers as partners

At home, collect items of rubbish that can be made into musical instruments. For example, two shampoo lids can be clapped together to make coconut shells; an upturned crisp tube or tin can become a small drum; a collection of milk bottle lids threaded onto a string can be jingling 'bells'; elastic bands stretched over a butter tub or a tissue box can become a 'guitar'. Have a musical session and march around in a marching band. Don't forget to sing!

Pirate party!

A pirate's life for me!

The final week of the topic is an opportunity to invite parents and carers into the setting to share some of the activities in which the children have been involved over the preceeding five weeks.

Tickell stated in her review that,

> 'Where parents and carers are actively encouraged to participate confidently in their children's learning and healthy development, the outcomes for children will be at their best'

It is crucial that parents and carers are involved and feel able to support their children at every stage of development. This final week is, therefore, a time for the children to celebrate their successes, perform some of their new skills for their families to see and for parents and carers to be involved in their learning.

In the week building up to inviting the parents and carers into the setting the children can be involved in making invitations, decorations, food and practising songs, drama and dances to share on the special day.

The actual event can be really flexible in length, style and amount of parental involvement. Depending on the setting and the number of children involved it is possible to make this event an hour or a day long, or you may need to repeat it for two different cohorts of children. It could simply be an open style morning or afternoon for people to drop in, to look at things the children have made, or be a mini concert, where the children can perform dances, sing songs for the parents and afterwards share food the children have produced.

Whatever the design, the purpose is to share some of the activities and crafts the children have been involved in, and to celebrate the topic of Pirates and Seaside.

Listed below are ideas for celebration linked to each of the seven areas of learning, along with some ideas for parental involvement and understanding. The detailed expected Early Learning Goal is also noted again here as a reminder of the expected level of attainment and understanding.

These are just some of the possible ideas – have fun, be creative and do whatever works for you and your children!

Ideas for a Pirate party

- Make invitations, cards and decorations – invitations to a beach picnic, make pirate and parrot masks, pirate hats or strings of gold coins to wear.

- Decorate the setting with some of the artwork produced – display the oceans in bottles; have an art corner and display the maps and plans of treasure islands in both 2D and 3D form.

- Eat special food – make some fruit salads and strangely shaped frozen ice lollies to share with the parents and carers, or bake some pirate biscuits cut into the shape of three cornered hats or boats.

- Dress up in special clothing – allow the children to wear their best party clothes, pirate costumes or seaside related fancy dress; decorate the children's faces with Jolly Roger flags painted onto their cheeks.

- Play party games – move like a pirate performing actions such as climbing the rigging, scrubbing the decks or looking out to sea; listen to some sea shanties, play the beach music and march around with some home-made instruments; wear pirate hats and fancy dress to parade around the setting.

Opportunities within Literacy

Aspect	Expected statements (ELGs)
Reading	Children read and understand simple sentences. They use phonic knowledge to decode regular words and read them aloud accurately. They also read some common irregular words. They demonstrate understanding when talking with others about what they have read.
Writing	Children use their phonic knowledge to write words in ways which match their spoken sounds. They also write some irregular common words. They write simple sentences which can be read by themselves and others. Some words are spelt correctly and others are phonetically plausible.

Most parents and carers are used to and comfortable with sharing books with children, as it is something that they have enjoyed regularly at home as their child has grown up. It's therefore a good idea to set up a corner within the setting with cushions, low tables and chairs to invite adults to sit quietly with the children reading, talking and listening. Put out a selection of books related to the topic, particularly including books that the children have seen before and which they have enjoyed in the setting. Include both fiction and non-fiction to appeal to a wide range of children and adults, and also include dual language texts. The children will relish being the expert when sharing the books with their parent or carer, and it gives a little quiet time to those finding the celebration a little busy.

Put out a writing area with a variety of suitable materials – include sticky labels, coloured sticky notes, postcards, envelopes, folded pieces of paper, lined, squared and dotted paper, old birthday or Christmas cards, old diaries and calendars and anything else the children would like to write upon! Include a mixture of pens, pencils and crayons. In this area also include blank invitations, picture holiday postcards, holiday travel brochures and seaside or beach pictures to colour, cut and stick – the children and adults can have fun writing to each other and making postcards or invitations. Children then see writing as having a purpose. If there are a variety of materials which are easily found in a home setting it may give ideas to the adults to encourage them to provide similar writing opportunities at home.

Opportunities within Mathematics

Aspect	Expected statements (ELGs)
Numbers	Children count reliably with numbers from 1 to 20, place them in order and say which number is one more or one less than a given number. Using quantities and objects, they add and subtract two single-digit numbers and count on or back to find the answer. They solve problems, including doubling, halving and sharing.
Space, shape and measures	Children use everyday language to talk about size, weight, capacity, position, distance, time and money to compare quantities and objects and to solve problems. They recognise, create and describe patterns. They explore characteristics of everyday objects and shapes and use mathematical language to describe them.

Let the children prepare for the adults visiting the setting by working out how many things will be needed for example: how many chairs altogether; how many around each table; how many cups or plates are needed? Setting the tables: have we enough; how many more; are they the same/equal? Extend this idea to the preparation of food when weighing for serving fruit or making fruit salad, or when buttering and cutting bread for sandwiches. Have a basket of pirate gold coins for the parents to 'spend' when they are buying an item for the picnic – can they help the children to count accurately?

Remind the children of the work they did making and reading their treasure maps and encourage them to make more maps, aging them by tearing edges and staining them with used teabags. Talk about the coloured patterns they used to make their flags and leave out a range of materials for them to replicate these patterns such as Unifix cubes and other construction equipment. Encourage them to challenge the adults to copy their patterns in different media.

These ideas are easily replicated at home, and the parents and carers can see how easy it is to provide simple mathematical activities at home without any special books or mathematical equipment.

Opportunities within Understanding the world

Aspect	Expected statements (ELGs)
People and communities	Children talk about past and present events in their own lives and in the lives of family members. They know that other children don't always enjoy the same things, and are sensitive to this. They know about similarities and differences between themselves and others, and among families, communities and traditions.
The world	Children know about similarities and differences in relation to places, objects, materials and living things. They talk about the features of their own immediate environment and how environments might vary from one another. They make observations of animals and plants and explain why some things occur, and talk about changes.
Technology	Children recognise that a range of technology is used in places such as homes and schools. They select and use technology for particular purposes.

Make a display of the photographs taken of the large scale boat that the children constructed from crates, ropes and tarpaulin. If there is room in the setting provide these large resources again so that the children can re-build their boats with the visiting adults. The children will enjoy talking about how they made their boat and what the different areas of the boat are for. If space is tight then provide the straws and materials for making model rafts, alongside the water tray so that they can be tested.

The use of ICT in the setting may be the most surprising to the parent and carer visitors. Ensure the computers and whiteboard are on (if you have them), digital cameras and voice recorders are available to use and toys such as programmable toys and pretend telephones and ovens are out for the children to show to the adults. Many parents and carers will believe that ICT relates only to computers: this is an opportunity to show them that technology includes the common objects in their own home.

A very simple but effective idea is to put all the photographs you have taken over the previous five weeks on as a slideshow – the children will love pointing themselves out, it is good evidence of the type of activities the children have been involved in and it will naturally prompt talk, listening and laughter.

Opportunities within Expressive arts and design

Aspect	Expected statements (ELGs)
Exploring and using media and materials	Children sing songs, make music and dance, and experiment with ways of changing them. They safely use and explore a variety of materials, tools and techniques, experimenting with colour, design, texture, form and function.
Being imaginative	Children use what they have learnt about media and materials in original ways, thinking about uses and purposes. They represent their own ideas, thoughts and feelings through design and technology, art, music, dance, role-play and stories.

Have an area set out as a place where adults and children can work together to produce decorations and artwork relevant to the topics looked at over the preceding five weeks. Provide paints for colour mixing to let the children show off their skills; put the chalks outside for the children to draw treasure maps on the floor; or provide brushes and water for the children to 'write' with outside on the ground. Providing simple pictures to colour (e.g. pirate pictures, boats and seaside scenes or shell patterns) is also a popular activity which many adults recognise, and may choose to sit alongside children and participate in without any fear of 'doing it wrong'.

If your setting allows for it, prepare an area with some musical instruments and possibly a CD player with some sea shanty type music. Let the children play the CD and investigate playing the instruments alongside. This activity works well outdoors, as there is more space for the children to march and move with the instruments. The increased space may also enable children to feel 'free' and you may find that they initiate an entire parade, making music and marching in time to the music! If you extend their opportunities by also providing masks, coloured scarves, flags, umbrellas, floaty sea type fabric and masks they are also more likely to develop characters within the music and begin to role-play quite naturally. Parents and carers can see from this that expensive character fancy dress sets are not necessary – with only a couple of old hats and scarves they can provide valuable opportunities at home for dressing up and firing the imagination of their child.

Opportunities within Communication and language

Aspect	Expected statements (ELGs)
Listening and attention	Children listen attentively in a range of situations. They listen to stories, accurately anticipating key events and respond to what they hear with relevant comments, questions or actions. They give their attention to what others say and respond appropriately, while engaged in another activity.
Understanding	Children follow instructions involving several ideas or actions. They answer 'how' and 'why' questions about their experiences and in response to stories or events.
Speaking	Children express themselves effectively, showing awareness of listeners' needs. They use past, present and future forms accurately when talking about events that have happened or are to happen in the future. They develop their own narratives and explanations by connecting ideas or events.

For some children who can find the setting a little overwhelming sharing their activities and successes with a familiar adult can be reassuring. They appreciate the time to be the expert, talking to their parent or carer about their daily activities and routines without the pressure to chat to a stranger or in front of others. For the practitioner in the setting this is also an ideal opportunity to listen quietly and unobtrusively to the child's conversation with others – it may be the first time you have heard the child speak!

Opportunities within Physical development

Aspect	Expected statements (ELGs)
Moving and handling	Children show good control and co-ordination in large and small movements. They move confidently in a range of ways, safely negotiating space. They handle equipment and tools effectively, including pencils for writing.
Health and self-care	Children know the importance for good health of physical exercise, and a healthy diet, and talk about ways to keep healthy and safe. They manage their own basic hygiene and personal needs successfully, including dressing and going to the toilet independently.

This can link quite closely with the music and movement idea in Expressive arts and design where the children can move confidently and with control around the outdoor environment. It is useful for the parents and carers to note that young children need to have opportunities for physical play or movement several times a day, whether it is walking to school or running around the local park or garden.

There are many activities which encourage fine motor skills, including threading bead jewellery to make pirate treasure; making flag patterns with coloured pegs and peg boards; building boats with construction equipment or using pencils to trace, write, draw and colour. Parents can extend this at home very simply without any special equipment, for example by threading penne pasta onto string to make jewellery; using clothes pegs to hang out the washing; playing with small construction equipment (e.g. Lego) or small world play (e.g. a doll's house) or cutting pieces of baking paper for children to place over the pictures in their colouring book to use as a cheap alternative to tracing paper. It is vital that parents recognise these pre-writing skills as crucial in a child's fine motor development.

To promote good health and self-care it is useful to have a large display where the children (but more importantly, the parents and carers) can see it, showing which children can achieve such things as using the toilet independently, washing their hands, putting on their own coat or fastening their own shoes. Maybe have small photographs of each child, and when they have achieved the target then their photograph is moved onto, for example, a large outline of a coat. These can be themed to match the topic, e.g. 'I can put on my pirate boots by myself.' The children in the setting will then be very aware of what they need to do, and will take this information home in the form of pester power – quickly learning how to perform the skill! Sometimes parents and carers do not realise what is necessary for their child to become more independent.

Opportunities within Personal, social and emotional development

Aspect	Expected statements (ELGs)
Self-confidence and self-awareness	Children are confident to try new activities, and say why they like some activities more than others. They are confident to speak in a familiar group, will talk about their ideas, and will choose the resources they need for their chosen activities. They say when they do or don't need help.
Managing feelings and behaviour	Children talk about how they and others show feelings, talk about their own and others' behaviour, and its consequences, and know that some behaviour is unacceptable. They work as part of a group or class, and understand and follow the rules. They adjust their behaviour to different situations, and take changes of routine in their stride.
Making relationships	Children play co-operatively, taking turns with others. They take account of one another's ideas about how to organise their activity. They show sensitivity to others' needs and feelings, and form positive relationships with adults and other children.

Within the six week topic block there are continual opportunities for children to demonstrate their development in the aspect of PSED. Each activity throughout the previous weeks requires children to work together, co-operate, talk about their ideas, choose resources and form positive relationships with others. This final opportunity for celebration allows the children to show that this positive behaviour is embedded, as the key skill of 'adjusting their behaviour to different situations and taking changes in routine in their stride' is certainly tested during this busy week.

Make a note of any children who have struggled with certain aspects of PSED and ensure that they are prepared for this change in routine: pair them with a particular friend for security; provide them with a quiet space (e.g. a tent, a book corner, even another room in the setting with another group) to which they can escape when it becomes too much; give them a

key responsibility to prevent idle hands (such as handing out biscuits to adults, collecting empty cups or even tidying pencils and putting away chairs) or simply ensure that they are your 'special helper' and that they are to stay with you throughout the event. This way you are building on the personal, social and emotional capabilities of your children and allowing them to develop further within a safe and structured environment.

Ensure most importantly that parents and carers understand the uniqueness of each child. Measuring their child's attainment, progress and temperament against that of another child is of no benefit whatsoever. A child who feels loved, supported and a valuable member of their early years community will grow and develop into an adult that is able to love and support others, and more importantly will be a valuable member of any community they choose to belong to throughout the rest of their life.

Observation record: Characteristics of Effective Learning

Name: _____ DoB: _____

Characteristics	Date	Activity observed	Evidence (What did you see?)
Playing and Exploring • Finding out and exploring • Playing with what they know • Being willing to 'have a go'			
Through active learning • Being involved and concentrating • Keeping trying • Enjoying achieving what they set out to do			
By creating and thinking critically • Having their own ideas • Making links • Choosing ways to do things			

Group record sheet for Communication and language (**prime**) and Literacy (**specific**)

Date completed _____

Children's names	Communication and language (prime)						Literacy (specific)			
	Listening and attention			Understanding		Speaking		Reading		Writing

Group record sheet for **prime** areas of learning (Personal, social and emotional development and Physical development) Date completed

Children's names	Personal, social and emotional development (prime)			Physical development (prime)	
	Self-confidence and self-awareness	Managing feelings and behaviour	Making relationships	Moving and handling	Health and self-care

Creative Planning in the EYFS © Lucy Peet

Group record sheet for **specific** area of learning (Mathematics)

Date completed _____

Children's names	Mathematics (specific)						Comments
	Numbers			Shape, space and measures			

Group record sheet for **specific** areas of learning (Understanding the world and Expressive arts and design)

Date completed _____

Children's names	Understanding the world (specific)									Expressive arts and design (specific)					
	People and communities			The world			Technology			Exploring and using media and materials			Being imaginative		

Planning overview: Pirates and the seaside (weeks 1 – 2)

Week	Main topic and activities	ELGs covered from specific areas of learning			
		Literacy *including some communication and language*	Mathematics	Understanding the world	Expressive arts and design
1	**Preparing to set sail** • What shall we take? • Maps and routes • Let's build a boat • Printing 'great waves'	Packing a tablecloth to take on our journey – can they remember everything that is packed? Children listen to stories, accurately anticipating key events and respond to what they hear with relevant comments, questions or actions. Children follow instructions involving several ideas or actions. Children use their phonic knowledge to write words in ways which match their spoken sounds. They also write some irregular common words. Some words are spelt correctly and others are phonetically plausible.	Using positional and directional language in making and reading a map, firstly in the small world and then onto paper. Using creasing, tearing and staining with cold teabags to make the maps look old. Children use everyday language to talk about size, weight, capacity, position, distance, time and money to compare quantities and objects and to solve problems. They recognise, create and describe patterns. They explore characteristics of everyday objects and shapes and use mathematical language to describe them.	Creating a large-scale role-play by building a boat, using large-scale construction including planks, crates, ropes and cloth tarpaulins. They can walking the plank and have water thrown at them! Children know about similarities and differences in relation to places, objects, materials and living things. They make observations of animals and plants and explain why some things occur, and talk about changes.	Looking at Hokusai's 'The Great Wave of Kanagawa' pictures, and printing their own versions. They safely use and explore a variety of materials, tools and techniques, experimenting with colour, design, texture, form and function. Children use what they have learnt about media and materials in original ways, thinking about uses and purposes. They represent their own ideas, thoughts and feelings through design and technology, art, music, dance, role-play and stories.
2	**Climb aboard** • Telescopes: 'I see a…' • Designing and making a flag • Will it float or sink? • Star constellations	Making and using a telescope to say and write simple sentences, beginning 'I see a…' Children listen attentively in a range of situations. Children express themselves effectively, showing awareness of listeners' needs. They use past, present and future forms accurately when talking about events that have happened or are to happen in the future. Children use their phonic knowledge to write words in ways which match their spoken sounds. They also write some irregular common words. They write simple sentences which can be read by themselves and others. Some words are spelt correctly and others are phonetically plausible.	Investigating patterns by using three colours to design a coloured flag, and investigating how many different ways there are to colour it. Children count reliably with numbers from 1 to 20, place them in order and say which number is one more or one less than a given number. They solve problems, including doubling, halving and sharing. Children use everyday language to talk about size, weight, capacity, position, distance, time and money to compare quantities and objects and to solve problems. They recognise, create and describe patterns. They explore characteristics of everyday objects and shapes and use mathematical language to describe them.	Using the water tray to investigate how much cargo a boat can carry before sinking. Children know about similarities and differences in relation to places, objects, materials and living things. They make observations of animals and plants and explain why some things occur, and talk about changes. Children recognise that a range of technology is used in places such as homes and schools. They select and use technology for particular purposes.	Looking at star constellations and making pictures and patterns of their own using black paper punched with holes. They safely use and explore a variety of materials, tools and techniques, experimenting with colour, design, texture, form and function. Children use what they have learnt about media and materials in original ways, thinking about uses and purposes. They represent their own ideas, thoughts and feelings through design and technology, art, music, dance, role-play and stories.

Planning overview: Pirates and the seaside (weeks 3 – 4)

Week	Main topic and activities	ELGs covered from specific areas of learning			
		Literacy including some communication and language	Mathematics	Understanding the world	Expressive arts and design
3	**Pirates ahoy!** • 'Wanted' posters • Pirate moneybags • Chilly pirate drinks • Pirate hats, cutlasses and eye patches	Making a 'wanted' poster for a pirate, drawing and adding labels to describe them. Children listen attentively in a range of situations. Children read and understand simple sentences. They use phonic knowledge to decode regular words and read them aloud accurately. They also read some common irregular words. They demonstrate understanding when talking with others about what they have read. Children use their phonic knowledge to write words in ways which match their spoken sounds. They also write some irregular common words. They write simple sentences which can be read by themselves and others. Some words are spelt correctly and others are phonetically plausible.	Using gold coins to count, add and exchange for treasure. Children count reliably with numbers from 1 to 20, place them in order and say which number is one more or one less than a given number. Using quantities and objects, they add and subtract two single-digit numbers and count on or back to find the answer. They solve problems, including doubling, halving and sharing.	Trying to keep an ice cube frozen by testing out different methods of insulation. Children know about similarities and differences in relation to places, objects, materials and living things. They make observations of animals and plants and explain why some things occur, and talk about changes.	Making a pirate hat, cutlass and eye patch from paper and card. They safely use and explore a variety of materials, tools and techniques, experimenting with colour, design, texture, form and function. Children use what they have learnt about media and materials in original ways, thinking about uses and purposes. They represent their own ideas, thoughts and feelings through design and technology, art, music, dance, role-play and stories.
4	**Treasure island** • Message in a bottle • Treasure map maths • Raft racing! • Pirate dancing	Writing a note to put in a bottle, to float off into the sea. Children listen attentively in a range of situations. They give their attention to what is being said to them and respond appropriately, while engaged in another activity. Children use their phonic knowledge to write words in ways which match their spoken sounds. They also write some irregular common words. They write simple sentences which can be read by themselves and others. Some words are spelt correctly and others are phonetically plausible.	Using coordinates to find treasure hidden under a cloth. Children count reliably with numbers from 1 to 20, place them in order and say which number is one more or one less than a given number. They solve problems, including doubling, halving and sharing. Children use everyday language to talk about size, weight, capacity, position, distance, time and money to compare quantities and objects and to solve problems.	Looking at different types of boat, and making a raft from straws. Children know about similarities and differences in relation to places, objects, materials and living things. They make observations of animals and plants and explain why some things occur, and talk about changes.	Making a pirate dance, by climbing the rigging, scrubbing the decks and looking for land ahoy! They safely use and explore a variety of materials, tools and techniques, experimenting with colour, design, texture, form and function. Children use what they have learnt about media and materials in original ways, thinking about uses and purposes. They represent their own ideas, thoughts and feelings through design and technology, art, music, dance, role-play and stories.

Creative Planning in the EYFS © Lucy Peet

Planning overview: Pirates and the seaside (weeks 5 - 6)

Week	Main topic and activities	ELGs covered from specific areas of learning			
		Literacy including some communication and language	Mathematics	Understanding the world	Expressive arts and design
5	**Sand and sea** • Beach safety poster • Making fruit salad • Ocean in a bottle • Beach music	Talking about safety on the beach, and making a poster showing how to keep safe. Children express themselves effectively, showing awareness of listeners' needs. They use past, present and future forms accurately when talking about events that have happened or are to happen in the future. They develop their own narratives and explanations by connecting ideas or events. They answer 'how' and 'why' questions about their experiences and in response to stories or events. Children use their phonic knowledge to write words in ways which match their spoken sounds. They also write some irregular common words. They write simple sentences which can be read by themselves and others. Some words are spelt correctly and others are phonetically plausible.	Cutting fruit into halves, quarters and thirds to share out and make fruit salad. Children count reliably with numbers from 1 to 20, place them in order and say which number is one more or one less than a given number. They solve problems, including doubling, halving and sharing. Children use everyday language to talk about size, weight, capacity, position, distance, time and money to compare quantities and objects and to solve problems.	Looking at the properties of oil and water, and using them to make an ocean in a bottle. Children know about similarities and differences in relation to places, objects, materials and living things. They make observations of animals and plants and explain why some things occur, and talk about changes.	Using natural materials found on a beach and percussion instruments to make beach music. Children sing songs, make music and dance, and experiment with ways of changing them. They represent their own ideas, thoughts and feelings through design and technology, art, music, dance, role-play and stories.
6	**Pirate party!**	Ideas to share with parents and carers			